Red Baron —
For the good ale days!

Blackie S.

Blackie Sherrod

AT LARGE

Blackie Sherrod

EAKIN PRESS ⬧ Austin, Texas

Most columns are from the *Dallas Morning News,* reprinted with permission, and from the now defunct *Dallas Times Herald.* All rights reserved. Cover photo by Jim Mahoney printed with permission of *Dallas Morning News.*

For CIP information, please access: www.loc.gov

FIRST EDITION
Copyright © 2002
By Blackie Sherrod
Published in the United States of America
By Eakin Press
A Division of Sunbelt Media, Inc.
P.O. Drawer 90159 ☎ Austin, Texas 78709-0159
email: sales@eakinpress.com
🖥 website: www.eakinpress.com 🖥
ALL RIGHTS RESERVED.
1   2   3   4   5   6   7   8   9
1-57168-721-1

Library of Congress Cataloging-in-Publication Data
Sherrod, Blackie.
    Blackie Sherrod at large / Blackie Sherrod.– 1st ed.
        p.   cm.
    Collection of articles from Dallas Morning News columnist,
Blackie Sherrod.
    ISBN 1-57168-721-1 (alk. paper)
    1. United States–History–1945–Anecdotes. I. Title.
E839.4 .S54 2002
973.92'02'07–dc21   2002014583

They tell me that book dedications are customary and even polite; therefore, this volume may as well be inscribed for The Geezers, a scruffy half-dozen wretches who know who they are and where and why. And who, after a zillion terms in pressboxes around the land, have a new Holy Grail to inspire them, that of finding a functional, affordable hearing aid.

Also by Blackie Sherrod

I Play to Win
Darrell Royal Talks Football
Scattershooting
The Blackie Sherrod Collection

Contents

The Media
Fourth Estate Follies and Fortes

Writers and Filmmakers
Purveyors of Inspiration and Sometimes Perspiration

This and That
Perspectives from an Armchair Sociologist

Sports
Lords of the Ring, the Field, and Other Venues

The Big, Wide World
War, Espionage, and Similar Issues of Global Importance

Preface

In the beginning, if you'll forgive a plagiarized opening, this hodgepodge of the printed word was destined to be titled "Beyond the Fence." This was a shameless theft of a premise by the late pressbox poet Red Smith, that he always tried to make his readers aware that he knew there was a world "beyond the outfield fence." That sports and the men who play them were not an end-all. That the infield fly rule, in final reckoning, ranks considerably below the Bill of Rights or the Battle of the Bulge.

However, after reviewing the following assemblage of columns, it was noticeable that a sports theme was indeed apparent in many of the offerings, even though they were published in other sections of newspapers. After a half-century in various games, it perhaps is only natural that jocktalk occasionally creeps, uninvited, into any subsequent essays. Osmosis, they call it over at the science building. Oh well.

Incredible Moments

When We All Stopped to Watch

Moonshot Experience Qualified as Science Fiction

(*Dallas Morning News,* July 21, 1994)

Harkback dispatches this week remind that it has been exactly one-quarter of a century since Norman Mailer and I covered the first moonshot.

It was a new experience, offering a journalistic springboard for both of us. One went on to broader horizons and international recognition. I don't know whatever happened to Mr. Mailer.

My presence at the Houston NASA center remains a mystery that Ms. Agatha Christie would die for, or at least get very ill. I was minding my own business, composing thoughtful essays on the infield fly rule and occasionally lecturing on Doak Walker at various social gatherings, when suddenly came a summons from the editor-in-chief.

The Big Cheese, after executive pondering, decided The Great Unwashed understood practically nothing about space travel. This moonshot surely was the greatest science story of all time, and The Great Unwashed didn't know it from fried okra.

So what was needed was a guileless reporter for the assignment. Whatever this dolt was able to understand enough to write about, the masses should be able to absorb. And what more helpless dolt on the subject than a sportswriter?

• • •

Before you could say Sir Isaac Newton, our man arrived in Houston and began research in approved journalistic fashion. I buttonholed the breakfast waitress at a hotel coffee shop. Name the three astronauts on Apollo 11, the demon reporter demanded.

"Goodness, I couldn't even name one, except maybe John Glenn," she said.

I tried another. "Who is Joe Namath?"

"Are you kidding?" says she. "He's the quarterback for the Jets. Didja want them eggs over easy?"

I remembered a few years before, when Gemini 11 was launched on a 72-hour orbit, a TV interviewer stopped a man on the street.

"Pardon me, sir, can you tell me who are Charles Conrad and Richard Gordon?" the reporter asked.

The fellow backed off and looked around him.

"I'm sorry, I'm a stranger in town," he said nervously. "I'm from Wichita, Kansas."

• • •

At least 2,500 science writers from around the globe sat with stereo headsets plugged into the conversations between Houston Base and Messers. Neil Armstrong, Buzz Aldrin and Mike Collins in the spacecraft.

Needless to say, I was the only guy there without a beard. These chaps conversed in unknown tongues of such gobbledegook as antipode, heliocentric, dislunar and ephemeris, which caused my eyes to cross.

Twice a day, in a massive auditorium, these science writers gathered for briefings from Chris Craft, the ground honcho. There were questions about something called El-Oh-Eye-One. The bloke in the next chair, with appropriate scorn, said it meant "the lunar orbit injection movement No. 1." This made me want to cry.

However, I was attracted to Mr. Armstrong because I learned he was opposed to jogging. His laconic dispatches from the capsule had all the animation of one of those guys on the weather channel. His normal pulse was in the high 60s, but when his foot touched the moon surface, no matter his apparent calm, his pulse was 156. I cornered a flight surgeon in private, where I wouldn't be embarrassed, and asked if that heartbeat was alarmingly high. He looked at me strangely.

"Well, we used to think so," he said finally. "But we ran some tests on race drivers waiting on the grid before the Indy 500 and found some pulses as high as 180."

4

Some beard said that Mr. Armstrong burned 3,625 British thermal units during his two hours on the moon. I asked and some beard figured out that was roughly the same energy spent by an NBA player during a game. Not bad for a 39-year-old non-jogger.

Oh, yes. Through dogged research, I discovered Mr. Armstrong carried a Civil Service rating of GS-16, Step 7, which specified an annual salary of $30,054. This meant he earned exactly $670.98 for being the first mortal to step on the moon, almost the amount Joe Namath spends on shoe shines.

That was about the extent of old buster's adventures on the moon. Norman Mailer? Well, he was on assignment from *Life* magazine. He came once to press headquarters and painstakingly took one sheet from each stack of official announcements and disappeared without a word.

However, I did not go on duty without professional preparation. We had a party at my house, and the 14 guests were asked to write down their No. 1 curiosity about the moonshot. Talk about thirst for scientific knowledge. Twelve asked the same question: How do they go to the bathroom up there?

Dallas' Dark Journey

(Dallas Morning News, November 22, 1988)

First of all, you must realize that the pressbox is the Plymouth Rock for all gallows humor as we know it today. There is no subject sacred to the biting lash of sports authors, not so much in their literary efforts but in their personal communication. Believe me, the pressbox was spewing sick humor around long before cable television.

And just as the wretches strive for toppers, also are they dedicated to stoicism. If a barb lodges under one's skin, one must never show it. One must be as the Spartan child who stole a fox, hid it under his tunic and when it began gnawing on his flesh, never changed expression lest it would give away his crime.

Those were the accepted pressbox mores in December 1963 when I walked into a hospitality suite at the Lexington Hotel in Manhattan. It was a sports trip, a gathering of All-America footballers and attending writers.

"Watch out, everybody!" yelled a man at the bar. "Here's that guy from Dallas! He's probably got a gun!"

The joker was an old newspaper pal from Georgia. The accepted reaction would have been to crouch at the knees, slap the hip in a swift draw. Instead, I got mad. Well, not exactly mad, but I felt a quick surge of resentment toward my friend. I felt my ears turning crimson, could actually feel the heat. The sense of dark humor had taken a leave of absence. I was utterly defenseless and I didn't like the feeling; I wanted to strike back but didn't know how. I felt ashamed and yet I was angry at myself for that feeling.

Now, looking back on those bewildering times, I realize that must have been the prevalent emotion that gripped the city in the immediate days after the assassination of President John F. Kennedy on that damned miserable November 22. Residents of Dallas, at least the overwhelming majority, were saddened by the rifle shots, certainly, but down deep inside, we also were resentful as hell that it happened here. Perhaps civic loyalists have a difficult time admitting that even today, but that's the way it was.

You see, this was new to the world. Today, cities could handle it. Today, people are hardened to sudden changes of history. We are still shocked, but the recovery time is far less. Forces go into immediate action and confusion is cut to a minimum, like grammar school pupils in a well-disciplined fire drill. Back then, it was a stunner. It was like Joe Louis banging you on the chin and, even if you didn't lose consciousness, you felt powerless to move. You could see and hear and smell, but you were maddeningly immobile.

Oh, proud Dallas historians might have you think the city rallied around, that astute leaders mounted their chargers and quickly began positive moves.

Not from where I sat, there in the newsroom of an afternoon paper.

It seemed to me that the brave, resolute commanders—and even many of us enlisted men—jutted our stalwart jaws, sprang to the saddle and rode determinedly off in all directions. We wanted desperately to defend the fort, but we didn't know the drill. We were the mother whose beloved son has been caught in the act of armed robbery. What can you say?

It was like menfolk at an old-timey country funeral. Women busied themselves inside the house, answering the phone, slicing the baked ham, tending the mourners. And the men gathered awkwardly in the yard, smoking, uncomfortable in starched collars and small talk. And a lady would call from the back porch, asking someone to fetch bread from the grocery and a dozen men would jump for their cars. They wanted action, wanted movement, wanted to demonstrate by their energies that they could be of use, could contribute to easing the day.

That's the way I remember that assassination aftermath. Nobody wanted to stand around and talk about it; everybody wanted to do something. It wasn't always the right thing. Nobody was real sure of the route to the grocery store. Those in the media were more fortunate than others. They stayed busy. Yet frequently they stepped out of character. I remember standing in the editor's office (watching the only television set on the floor), reporters sitting on the carpet, leaning against the wall, when the announcer gave the definite news that the president indeed was dead. I heard a gasp, and a male reporter was sobbing. I had never seen that before.

Late the next night, those on the midnight watch heard fearful screams from somewhere down the corridors. Understand, the assassination brought nuts out of the woodwork like earthworms after a rain. We had zany newsroom visitors who shouted and threatened and had to be removed forcibly. So screams in the night were not exactly out of mode.

Reporters scattered at high lope, each seeking the source. Finally, it was traced. A veteran pressman was trapped on stairs between floors. The door he entered locked behind him, the door he sought was locked in front of him. So he screamed at the top of his voice, really terrified shrieks. A week earlier, he would never have done that. A week later, it would have embarrassed him to tears. But now, when the door was opened to free him, he said not a word, just walked off to his press-room station.

Merriman Smith, the senior White House correspondent, came to our office to write and file his assassination coverage for United Press International. He was a calm, white-haired professional and it was most impressive when he finished, boarded the elevator and said, as the door closed, "Big D is Little D now."

Those who heard him resented it, mostly because we feared that would be the international opinion. Yet some of us have long held the theory that Jack Ruby's shooting of Lee Harvey Oswald—more than the assassination—was the absolute crusher for the Dallas image, if we may call it that.

On Sunday in Washington, the riderless horse and the muffled drums (you would never, never forget that drum beat) were escorting the president's coffin to the Capitol. And in the basement of the City Hall, Ruby was shooting Oswald in the left side with a .38-caliber Colt. Were it not for Ruby's act, the assassination might not have been so damning for the city. The town might have escaped as "a victim of circumstance," like Buffalo, N.Y., where William McKinley went down, and the Washington depot where James Garfield was shot, mere happenstance locations that did not add to nor subtract from the happening itself.

But then the Ruby slaying pulled the plug. In the City Hall basement, can you believe it! This became the Dallas black eye that no amount of brave cosmetics could disguise. And to compound it all, the mystery of Oswald died with him and the speculation kept, and still keeps, the subject dreadfully alive.

I remember an FBI agent, a friend of mine, coming to the newspaper office late Friday night of the assassination, to inspect all photographs shot by our lensmen that day, seeking any background face or anything that might be a clue as to Oswald's motive. He cursed Oswald, looked over his shoulder and muttered confidentially.

"I wish they'd let us have him for a few hours," he said. "We'd shoot his ass full of sodium pentothal and find out what's going on."

Instead the question remains in history, like the hulk of the USS *Arizona* in the shallow waters of Pearl Harbor, oil still seeping to the surface, a subject to be brought down from the shelf and dusted and polished every decade or so.

To Dallas old-timers, the tragedy has become like a birthmark on your child's face. The blemish is there, but you have become accustomed to it so that it is no longer a constant heartache. Not until a stranger remarks about it, that is; not until you drive past the old School Book Depository and see tourists staring at the sixth-floor window and unstrapping their Kodaks. And you still feel, however faintly, that stir of resentment and you realize again that the day and its shadow will never be forever erased from memory.

Bomb Sight

(*Dallas Morning News,* August 7, 1985)

Oddly enough, ferric oxide were the first words to come to mind. Ferric oxide. Iron rust. The barren Hiroshima countryside, its view filtered through plexiglass, seemed smothered in iron rust.

Frankly, I remembered the formula as *ferris* oxide, but then I had never been much of a chemistry student. I always had trouble remembering whether there were two parts hydrogen or two parts oxygen in a chaser. But now, for some inexplicable reason, the words ferris oxide popped into my mind and nested there, to be dislodged Tuesday when stories marked the 40th anniversary of the first atomic bomb drop. The memory struggled back through cobwebs of long tenure. I can't remember where I parked the car today, but some of *those* impressions are indelible.

This was a matter of a few days after the bomb had leveled some place called Hiroshima. (At the time, we pronounced it HEE-roe-sheema, and we didn't know it from Copenhagen.) I can't remember the exact day of our Hiroshima visit; my old Navy flight log is hazy about details, and besides, we weren't supposed to be there in the first place.

We were on an aimless mission, some admiral's son, en route to Japan immediately after the surrender, never made it, and several carrier search patrols were dispatched to seek any sign of seaplane wreckage or a rubber dinghy on beaches of Ryukyu Islands, off the tail of Japan. There were two of us in the TBM torpedo bomber, the pilot and young buster here in the belly.

The pilot came on the intercom. "You wanta go over to the main island and see where that big bomb hit the other day?" he asked. "The area is off-limits but we might sneak a quick look." The pilot was a harum-scarum lieutenant from South Dakota, Bill Majerus, and he cared little for regulations even though he was executive officer of the torpedo squadron.

Why not? Really, the curiosity was not that acute. So somebody dropped a couple of science fiction eggs and the war suddenly was over. Bombs are bombs, some are bigger than others, so what. So let's get home and see if we can find some ham and redeye gravy and grits.

The turret gunner had remained aboard ship that day, so I crawled up in his bubble for a better view. Majerus swooped down to, oh, maybe 400 feet, so that any view was fleeting and scrambled. The dominant impression was of ferric oxide, not the deep color of iron rust, but a faded shade. Not a pastel hue, pleasant to the eye. This was a harsh color, harsh and pale at the same time. As far as you could see in that hasty moment, everything wore that same dead, depressing blanket.

Not that there was a lot to see. The scene sweeping past the turret was mostly flat desolation, and there seemed amazingly little rubble. It hadn't been cleaned up yet; there had not been time. But perhaps most of the rock and wood, along with many of the inhabitants, had simply disintegrated or melted and left this pale red ash.

There would be an occasional wall standing, maybe one in an area of what would be five city blocks. No wrecked building, merely a bare stone wall, forlorn and useless. Unbelievably, there were trees! There was an occasional tree, or the skeleton thereof, stripped of any sign of foliage, a scarecrow of a tree, pale red like its background.

There seemed to be a strange odor, permeating even the turret of a rushing aircraft, a sort of musty smell, like of old houses, dark and shuttered against the outside, furniture squatting under sheets. But that could have been a young imagination, and probably was.

We were aware of no living creature or plant. Probably there were scattered work crews, or maybe the whole area was isolated because of the danger of fallout, if indeed we knew about fallout at that time. But we saw nothing but a vast, flat wasteland covered with this pale red dust. The pilot made only two quick runs and then got the hell out of there. There was

11

perhaps 15 minutes of silence as the plane pointed back toward the task force somewhere over the horizon.

Majerus broke it. "Well, that was something, wasn't it?" his voice came into the earphones.

Indeed it was, but we did not know exactly what and somehow the curiosity was not overwhelming. Just days previously, at the time "Little Boy" was dropped on Hiroshima, our air group was staying at a bleak airstrip on Saipan. When a carrier makes port or anchors offshore, its planes fly off beforehand and set up at the nearest airstrip. This is so, in event of submarine or air attack, the motionless carrier is not caught with its planes on deck, unable to launch same.

For several days, we had watched these huge B-29s take off from Tinian, a sister island perhaps three miles west. We were awed by the size of these huge silver cigars, because ours was a world of short, chunky carrier planes. The morning of August 7, gunners were called to a Quonset hut for an unusual briefing by the air group intelligence officer, a young and rather nervous chap. He said he didn't know a lot, didn't have many details, but the previous day, a B-29 from neighboring Tinian had dropped something called an "atom bomb" on Japan, and the devastation was so vast that surely Japan would be surrendering within a matter of days.

"A whole city was leveled, the way we understand it," said the briefing officer. "Hundreds of thousands of people killed." Well, we knew something about bombs. The TBM bay would hold a 2,000-pound torpedo or a 2,000-pound bomb, and it could raise considerable ruckus. But an entire city with just one bomb?

The first question was, how big was this rascal? "As I understand, it's about the size of a walnut," said the young officer. "It has something to do with atoms expanding, some sort of chain reaction."

We stared at him. (As we later learned, the first atom bombs were big as a small barn.) The walnut was beyond belief, except at that time so were many other subjects. So nobody worried much about it, nor talked much about it when the USS *Santee* recalled her planes and wallowed north toward the defeated land.

Somebody had done run in a Buck Rogers war on us, and if it got things over in a hurry, well, bully for them. And if you could look up the remnants of that group and ask about the walnut that turned Hiroshima into a pale red desert 40 years ago, I think you'd find they thought it came in mighty handy.

Bomb Wasn't a Moral Issue to Troops in the Pacific

(*Dallas Morning News,* August 3, 1995)

It may come as a surprise to you that I have not always been wise, or even smarter than the average frog. This is not an easy admission, what with all these Vaunted Experts currently permeating the media. In these twilight years, I yearn for the mantelletta of a pundit in an ivory tower, writing with great authority on topics other than red-eye gravy and Babe Ruth.

No such luck. As a youth, I was frequently overcome with slow wit, and now it appears the affliction has lingered, just under the surface, ready for instant recall.

It was not until this August 6 fuss rumbled to prominence like a sulfuric belch that realization of my ignorance struck home. Apparently it requires wisdom far beyond my ken to understand all this pompous second-guessing about the atomic bomb a half-century ago.

The 50th anniversary of the Hiroshima bombing has lured countless gurus from their mountaintops to pass ponderous judgment in retrospect. Television specials somberly question the "morality" of the act. There is uproar against a Hiroshima postage stamp and *Enola Gay* display in the Smithsonian Institution. There is sentiment to offer a public apology to Japan. Many of these esteemed moralists have issued edicts branding Harry Truman "a savage" for OKing the drop. One historian termed the president a "racist."

Gallup pollsters report most younger Americans deem it was wrong to drop the atomic bomb, that it was immoral and unnecessary. Obviously these are far wiser younguns than we were at comparable ages.

• • •

In immediate aftermath of that 1945 August day, I don't recall any protest marches. We were told that the one

Hiroshima bomb destroyed a Japanese city. But then, Gen. Curtis LeMay's B-29 firebombers had been doing the same thing for weeks, leveling 32 square miles and four cities in one 10-day stretch. It just took them longer. The new bomb struck us as a mere speed-up process.

Mainly our emotion was one of relief, bovine as we were. As it happened, a tailhook group of my acquaintance was camping on a scruffy Saipan airstrip while its carrier was being restocked off-shore. Each morning, guys watched the tubular silver B-29s take off from Tinian, three miles across a channel, and head for Japan, 1,600 miles north. *Enola Gay* had left from that runway.

Scuttlebutt had our particular bunch joining a task force for invasion of Japan in mid-autumn. Someone ventured a landing in a place named Korea, a name few had ever heard before. (Later, of course, they learned the invasion was pointed at the southern island of Kyushu and that Japan had amassed 500,000 troops there, plus 5,000 kamikazes, in anticipation of same.)

Remembering the grim tenacity of Japanese defense of little spots like Iwo Jima and Okinawa, one could only wonder at the ferocity with which these people would defend their homeland. The kamikaze suicide planes are prime example. Even the dumbest dogface and swab jockey realized it was not going to be boring.

• • •

To our slow, perhaps selfish, reasoning, the A-bomb not only sped things up but spared a great many lives on both sides. As for "inhumanity" and "immortality," the subject never came up. Frankly, had we been asked, we would have been hard pressed to find great *morality* in the London buzz bombs, for that matter, or the Bataan Death March or Buchenwald. In combat, the common bloke has little time for philosophy; his scope goes only to the horizon.

In this later-day forum, this spasm of second-guessing, we

try to explain our lack of compassion by saying it all depends on who you are and where and when.

However, there is another memory of that day, 50 years past. Word of Hiroshima was accompanied with prophecy that all cannons would soon be stilled. Some humane gold braid, in honor of the occasion, authorized two humane cans of beer for each enlisted man. The beer was tepid, a condition we remedied by good old Yankee ingenuity, chilling the cans with CO_2 foam from flightline fire extinguishers. We weren't dumb in all matters.

You Always Will Remember Where You Were

(*Dallas Morning News,* September 12, 2001)

Within the geezerhood, there will be immediate hark-backs to December 7, 1941. There is an indelible memory of the Sunday noon—where we were, what the weather was like, what we were wearing, how we heard the news of the Japanese dawn attack on our Pacific Navy base.

Today, we can't remember a wedding anniversary, but those whiskery particulars of long ago stay with us like a tattoo. And we also remember there was one predominant question among most of us naive youngsters at the time: Where, what and even who was Pearl Harbor?

Back then, even as you pulled on your clothes, backed the roadster out of the driveway and rattled downtown to your new job as a rookie reporter on a small Texas newspaper—never even thinking about Sunday being your day off—you wondered how this could happen to big, old, strong us.

This, of course, will be your—our—experience of September 11, 2001. Much of it will be the same; only these memories will be even more graphic, more realistic. It will be more believable, less surprising to the old grunts.

This time you were shaving, perhaps, or preparing the kids for school or having coffee in the kitchen with the television furnishing incidental background. Take it from the graybeards, you will remember. And some of you will wonder in disbelief how this could happen to big, old, strong us.

In 1941, we were surprised that an attack would come from Asia; we would not have been shocked had it come from Europe. This time, we really shouldn't be all that stunned at the origin. Nor at the form of attack.

In 1941, the target was military. That old rulebook has been discarded. Can you believe, one day back there in the Pacific, that Navy airmen had their Smith & Wesson .32

sidearms confiscated and were issued Colt .45s instead? The given reason: The S&Ws used lead bullets, which were against the Geneva Convention. Honest, that's what we were told.

Today, there are no rules, no conventions. What we have are suicidal attackers. We fight shadows who are convinced they have nothing to lose. The only thing to expect is the unexpected.

There seems two major differences between December 7, 1941, and September 11, 2001.

First, we are much more informed. Before the echo of the first World Trade Center explosion died, there were pictures on your TV screen. You knew exactly when, where and how. You had reporters and cameramen roaming New York streets, stopping fleeing survivors with the stock question: "What was going through your mind?" There on your screen, with the Pentagon burning in the background, senators and congressmen offered expert opinions. "Unbelievable!" they said. Maybe that was the trouble with our preparation. We refused to believe that the unbelievable was real.

And then—the biggest difference of all. For the great majority of U.S. residents, their last half-dozen wars or "police actions" have been remote affairs, conducted by a relatively few citizens on foreign ground. Not since the Civil War has our own precious countryside been so scarred and our innocent civilians slain.

Old vets may say, without bitterness, that most Americans never really have experienced war. Oh, they might have had shortages, blackouts and relatives at risk. But they never actually were in war, not like the Brits, who huddled in nighttime basements and pulled dead relatives and children from bomb rubble, or the bloody folk in Berlin, for that matter, or on the Russian ice or in Manila or Nagaski. U.S. commonfolk mostly watched from the upper balcony.

Now that's changed. This nation's populace is itself involved. And in the final reckoning, that may be the major difference between December 7, 1941, and September 11, 2001.

Incredible People

And the Mark They Left

The Mechanical Man

(Dallas Times Herald, July 21, 1969)

Neil Armstrong has been pictured as the first robot to step on the moon.

He is the coldly efficient astronaut, the silent loner who operates by the numbers. Other heroes calm their stomachs by swinging a golf club or dealing a few in the back room. Neil Armstrong prefers to climb in a glider and sail off in solitary quietness.

The Apollo 11 commander lives in a 39-year-old armor and he never uses a word when a shrug will do. This flight to the moon was universally judged the most uncommunicative trip of the ten-year space program. When the mission boss did speak—and many times he had to be prompted by ground officials—it was terse technicalities.

On telecasts from the speeding capsule en route, Armstrong usually held the camera and focused attention on teammates Buzz Aldrin and Mike Collins. When he got the final okay for the actual moon landing, the Armstrong "roger" was as emotional as a fry cook acknowledging an order for two over easy.

But the mechanical man took a stoolpigeon along on the jaunt and got himself unmasked as mortal flesh and nerves. Armstrong's heartbeat was the tattletale. Sensor wires taped to his left ribs signaled Armstrong's emotions a quarter-million miles to nosey parkers in NASA headquarters. His expression might have been poker-faced, but his pulse was not.

Just before the skinny legs of the lunar vehicle touched the foreign gray dust, Armstrong's heartbeat more than doubled its normal rate. His pulse shot up to 156 thumps a minute. Try that on your old triphammer. Usually Armstrong's heart is clocked in the low 70s.

His voice was flat and steady as ever, but you can't fool the old ticker.

• • •

Several days before the landing, some disappointed journalist wondered if Armstrong finally would show some human expression in his first words from the moon proper.

"I imagine he'll just call Houston and say he's landed," said flight director Cliff Charlesworth. He tagged it on the button. There was a flurry of technical transmissions as the moonship hovered over the surface and then Armstrong's rather high-pitched drone:

"Houston, Tranquility Base here. The Eagle has landed."

The Sea of Tranquility was the landing spot in moon geography; Eagle was the name of the craft. Armstrong might have been telling his wife that the babysitter had arrived.

Dr. Thomas Payne, administrator of the entire space operation, wasn't fooled. Of course, he had a clue from Dr. Charles Berry, the chief flight surgeon who was monitoring Armstrong's innards.

"Medical indications were very clear that although the voice was under tight control, his emotion was running rather high, as it was in all of us, "said Dr. Payne.

One cause of Armstrong's rapid rate might have been the small emergency that developed just before landing. The spaceship seemed headed, by automatic guidance, toward a rocky crater. Armstrong had to switch to manual control and steer the thing the dickens out of there to an open pasture.

It was a particularly soft landing for the four-footed critter, but it still was a long ways from home and the very first time anybody used the moon for anything but a song title.

"I wasn't surprised at Neil's pulse rate," said Dr. Berry. "Heck, I thought it would be a hundred and eighty."

• • •

It was possible to monitor just one of the Eagle's passengers in flight. Aldrin's pulse wasn't recorded until he got out of the ship and began his ghostly ballet on the moon. Both astronauts' heartbeats slowed to the 90s during their two-hour walk.

22

"Considerably slower than mine," said Charlesworth with a laugh.

Then came another hint as to the mechanical man's humanness. Dr. Berry remembered back to Armstrong's previous flight, Gemini 8. It was supposed to be a three-day affair, but a power system went haywire and pitched the craft into an unnatural spin. Armstrong had to abandon the flight plan and bring the ship to an emergency landing in the Pacific, instead of a less hurried splashdown in the Atlantic.

"I don't remember exactly how high his pulse went then," said Dr. Berry. "Something over one-forty. Not as high as this time. But that's not critical. We have purposely raised guys to one-eighty and kept them there for a while."

Col. Paul Campbell, former head of aerospace medicine for the Air Force, was with the astronaut program from the first days.

"You know, when we first started having manned flights, we had astronauts whose pulses went up to one-forty at launch. Sometimes more. People said, you can't do that. Their hearts can't stand it. It's never been done.

"Then somebody ran the same test on Indianapolis race drivers while they were on the grid, just before the race started," said the colonel. "They found even higher pulses than astronauts. We didn't hear any more about it."

• • •

Armstrong was to pound even more blood. At the end of his moon exercise, when he was hoisting boxes of rock specimens into the spacecraft, his heartbeat reached 160.

"But he was doing a lotta work then," said the flight surgeon.

Once back through the narrow hatch in his bulky spacesuit (a chore in itself without excitement or previous exercise) the boyish-faced Armstrong resumed his calm, normal pulse. But the mechanical man already had been stripped of his shell. Only his heartbeat knew for sure.

23

From the Top of the Stairs

(*Dallas Times Herald,* August 17, 1970)

This was a corridor deep in the muggy innards of Comiskey Park and it was jammed to the crummy walls with miserable bodies, shoving, shouting, impatient to be about their business. A huge guard with a prow like the USS *Missouri* blocked the way to Floyd Patterson's dressing room door. All he needed was a broadax and you would have placed him outside the sultan's bedroom. Patterson had just lost his title to Sonny Liston in the first round and us pressbox wretches had been stalled outside his portals for almost an hour, while Patterson struggled with his composure and deadlines flittered away into the midnight hours.

Suddenly the guard shouted, "Stand back!" and there was a new wave of shoving. The door was wedged open and the guard hacked a path for two people to leave. One was Patterson's mother, and her escort was a slight dapper gent in a splendid white raincoat, serenely calm as he guided the woman through the irate masses. When the horde squeezed inside, Patterson had already ducked out the back way. Only one guy had his story, and that was the dapper gent in the raincoat, Doc Greene, the implausible columnist from Detroit who was forever appearing in implausible places.

Once when Ingemar Johansson and his brother were fishing on a remote stream in Lapland, miles from civilization, they heard a car brake on a nearby road. Minutes later, implausible Doc Greene walked out of the woods and said hi.

We were covering the Masters a few years back when I found a packet in my hotel box one morning. Doc had left some clubhouse drink chit books with a note explaining he had to charter a plane and get somewhere in the Caribbean. A friend had called him during the night with an invitation to go scuba diving and that sure as hell, he said, beat listening to Gary Player talk about eating raisins to give him strength. In fact, that was exactly how we spent the day before, listening to Gary Player talk about raisins. Doc had turned slowly, raised one eyebrow a sixteenth of an inch, and ordered a gin and tonic. Without raisins. Getting the scuba invite was like hearing from the governor.

• • •

Implausible Doc Greene wrote columns about implausible people in sports—a stablehand, a boccie bowler, a world champion belly-bumper, a lizard racer, mountain climbers, and Joe Frisco. Gad, how he loved Stuttering Joe Frisco, the horse-player. His favorite Frisco story was the time when the little loser borrowed fifty bucks from Bing Crosby at Santa Anita. A couple hours later, Joe had his five straight winners. He was holding court at the clubhouse bar when Crosby walked in and eyed him significantly. Frisco jerked a fifty from a pile of ban-knotes on the bar and waved it grandly at Crosby.

"Here, b-b-oy," he said loudly, "g-g-give us a chorus of White Christmas."

Doc would type out these idylls in the wee hours, after the pressrooms were deserted, squinting through his cigarette smoke and deliberately pressing one key at a time. He was the all-time fop, ever at the peak of fashion, pink shirts, high white tab collars, gleaming cuffs with huge links, glistening shoes, never a hair out of place, never a bead of sweat, never a quick, hurried motion. He even had a high-fashion head, sleek and a bit weary, and his eyes bugged slightly like his tie might be too tight. He looked to be made of Dresden. Not many knew he carried a sprinkling of Japanese lead and he had the Navy Cross and a few other bangles in some obscure drawer, souvenirs of Pacific days as a Marine platoon leader. He was a novice bullfighter in Mexico and a professional actor and a casino stick man and he once ran a harness track.

When he went to Florida for spring baseball training, none of this hotel business with us other slobs. Doc rented a houseboat.

He married Miki, a pretty soft blonde pal who had been Miss Florida.

25

"She won it in 1957," Doc would say gently. "It was not a vintage year."

. . .

Probably the nearest Doc ever came to frantic motion was one year at the Preakness. He was due back in Detroit at 8 P.M. because a couple friends were getting married in his apartment. His commercial airline connections from the Washington airport were close enough, but an inquiry held up the Preakness result even longer. Doc pulled a fistful of winnings from his pocket, called a helicopter service, had a chopper land in the Pimlico infield. He strode regally across the track, climbed aboard, and the machine whirred off above the impressed crowd to the Washington airport.

Ill health had plagued Doc for the past few years. He was not exactly like the old lady of the Mark Twain story, the one who led such an exemplary life that when she became ill, she had no bad habits to give up, to help her back to health.

"She was like a sinking ship," said Twain, "with no freight to throw overboard."

Doc had plenty habits to discard, but he fought most of them off. At the 1964 U.S. Open in Washington, he was on the wagon. "I have to go to the hospital for a checkup," he said. "They won't take me unless I haven't had a drink for eleven straight days."

"I've almost made it a couple times," he sighed. "Got up to nine once."

This time he was determined to endure the 11-day drouth. We went to Trader Vic's for pressed duck and he introduced me to Navy grog. Said it had always been his favorite Polynesian medicine, and he watched closely as I made its acquaintance. The first one was tall and cool and delicious and quite enough.

"No," Doc said enviously, raising a finger to the waiter. "That one was for me. Now have one for yourself."

A heart attack done him in Wednesday. He left word, said Miki, that don't none of you bums send flowers. If you must do something, send a book to the Detroit library. He had style.

Amateurs Shouldn't Try This Trick

(Dallas Morning News, May 8, 1997)

By his own admission, Leo Durocher was the keenest judge of baseball talent. Ask the old sharpie the best player he ever saw, and he didn't hesitate.

"Willie Mays," he would say promptly. Then he always would cut himself a backdoor.

"Unless," he'd say, "it was Pete Reiser."

None but the most astute baseball students will place the name. Were it not for injury, Pete Reiser would rank in every top drawer. The Dodger could do it all. Trouble was, Mr. Reiser was always running full tilt into fences or dugouts or hindcatchers and fracturing some vital bone or knocking himself silly. Like Jack Kennedy, Mr. Reiser went down in history as the Magnificent Maybe.

However, the reason I was a fan of Mr. Reiser's is that he taught me the best card trick I ever knew.

First off, I am a sucker for card tricks or, in fact, any sleight of hand. Never mind these "illusionists" like this Copperfield fellow or Siegfried & Roy or the chaps who make a billygoat appear in your fireplace. These fellows use mirrors and wires and trapdoors while flitting about the stage like a ballet dancer. But sleight-of-handers are craftsmen, not electricians.

• • •

I first knew Pete Reiser when he managed a minor league team in the Dodger chain. In spring training, after dinner, managers and coaches and press wretches would gather in a large room at the rear of the camp cafeteria, play cards and tell lies and such. It was there Mr. Resier taught me that intricate card trick. There was a narrative involved, but I memorized it, and back home, I was the life of the party at the tables down at Morey's or wherever good fellows gather.

Somewhere along the line, I got tied up solving world problems and, after a year or so, discovered I had forgotten the trick. A decade passed before I ran across Mr. Reiser at some winter baseball banquet, sat him down and made him review the act. This time I wrote it down, step by step, in a notebook that, with the grace of long practice, I proceeded to lose. Shortly after, Mr. Reiser died, leaving me adrift.

Which brings us, at long last, to my favorite card trick or, rather, the story of same.

John Scarne was one of the foremost card mechanics of all time, internationally recognized. He also was a prizefight fan and a close pal of Jimmy Braddock's, the former heavyweight champ. They made most of the big fights, and it was before the Sonny Liston-Floyd Patterson bout in Chicago that I was exposed to Mr. Scarne.

He visited the Hilton pressroom to see an old friend, Doc Greene of Detroit, a typist who was not adverse to games of chance. Mr. Scarne was a stocky middle-aged chap with a cigar stub in his face. He would fetch a greasy deck of cards from somewhere in a rumpled gray suit and, with fingers thick as bratwursts, entertain for hours.

"Tell them about the best trick you ever did," Doc Greene said one night. Mr. Scarne needed no prompting.

• • •

He was a young lad in Chicago, working the small clubs. Frequently mobsters were in the audience. For some reason, mobsters dearly love card tricks and often hired the sharps to amuse them at private functions.

This particular night, some Detroit peers were visiting their Chicago counterparts, deciding who needed shot and whatever. The Chicago hosts hired young Mr. Scarne to entertain.

The site was a luxury suite on the ground floor of a suburban motel, with a full glass wall overlooking the city. A heavy rain was pelting the glass, providing a mysterious background when Mr. Scarne did his number. He had the Detroit boss select a card, say the eight of diamonds, hide it in the deck and shuffle thoroughly. Then Mr. Scarne took the cards, shuffled again and suddenly threw the deck against the glass wall. One card stuck to the glass. The eight of diamonds.

"Aw, what kind of a trick is that?" said the Detroit visitor. "Any punk could do that." The Chicago hosts were embarrassed and glared heavily at the young cardsharp.

"Well, bring the card to me," said Mr. Scarne, "and I will do something else with it."

Still sneering, the Detroit mobster guy got up and went to the glass wall to fetch the stuck card. In vain. The eight of diamonds was on the outside of the window.

With Hogan, There Was No Unforeseen

(*Dallas Morning News,* July 31, 1997)

At the airport last week, when young Justin Leonard returned from the British Isles, there were 400 cheering souls to greet him. A thousand more awaited at his country club.

At another airport 44 years ago, another British Open champion came home, and a half-dozen of us waited at the corridor stairs. There wasn't even a photographer, just some businessmen, a neighbor or so and a brace of Fort Worth newspaper cubs.

Although he was renowned for stoicism, Ben Hogan seemed a bit nonplused. He was genuinely surprised, and a bit embarrassed, that anyone would take the trouble.

There was a sort of awkward moment, until Mr. Hogan led his wife, Valerie, to the side, where they stood, shook hands and thanked each well-wisher for his presence.

• • •

That scene returned to memory when Mr. Hogan's death hit the weekend wires. This was not a surprise, for word of his illness had been passed for the last few years. It was symbolic of the Hogan mystique that no one spoke of the illness in a loud voice, only in the hushed tones one uses at a funeral. It was as though he were standing there with a withering glance, ready to sear anyone who spoke aloud of a physical weakness.

This being the Hogan image, that of a cold, stoic person very much in control of all he surveyed, that scene at Amon Carter Field is all the more memorable. The fellow seemed genuinely flustered at the unexpected attention, even from such a few. It was something he had not prepared for, and the Ben Hogan of legend was prepared for anything.

In that respect, he was like the late Leo Durocher. One spring, the Dodger manager outlined to reporters his club's prospects in great detail.

"But, Leo, what if the unforeseen happens?"

Mr. Durocher glared at the questioner. "There ain't gonna be no unforeseen!" said he.

That was the particular aura around Mr. Hogan. He would not allow no unforeseen.

• • •

There was another time when the little golfer was caught short, but it was not apparent to witnesses. The year the Salesmanship Club named its tournament the Byron Nelson Classic, there was a pre-tournament dinner honoring Mr. Nelson. It probably was the grandest sports banquet I ever attended, and there have been hundreds. They were all there, Palmer, Nicklaus, Player, Casper, De Vicenzo, Floyd, Jacklin, the Heberts, Jack Fleck and Vic Ghezzi, for goodness sakes, scattered throughout the audience. I sat at a table with Mason Rudolph and Don January. Chris Schenkel emceed.

Mr. Hogan agreed to attend—the secret word was—only on conditions he not be asked to speak. Mr. Hogan and Mr. Nelson learned their trade together, starting as caddies at Glen Garden Country Club, but they weren't bosom pals. Mutual respect and all that, but they were opposite personalities: Mr. Nelson, outgoing, gracious, friendly to all; Mr. Hogan, almost a silent recluse.

At any rate, on this night Mr. Hogan preferred to leave the Nelson plaudits to others and not to impose his particular presence on a night honoring his peer.

• • •

Jimmy Demaret would have none of it. Mr. Demaret was the jovial bon vivant of golfdom, perhaps the only one who could joke and tease Mr. Hogan.

Anyway, Mr. Demaret was introduced, sang a song, then grabbed the mike and demanded Mr. Hogan come to the stage and say a few words about his fellow townsman. Mr. Hogan shook his head firmly, but the applause became so prolonged that finally he left his table and went to the stage. He shot Mr.

Demaret a look that seared the buttons on his shorts, then proceeded to make the neatest little off-the-cuff talk I ever heard, even a little sentimental, about how he and Valerie and Byron and Louise survived the early, threadbare days on the tour. Each of the several anecdotes had a deft illustrative point.

Those are the foremost Hogan memories prompted by his death. There are others not quite as pleasant. He could charm, and he could frost. He did not suffer fools gladly. It would have been interesting, and perhaps a little historic, had the fellow been a part of today's hectic arena.

Arizona Heroes Aren't Unlikely Pair

(*Dallas Morning News,* June 11, 1998)

The hunch here, admittedly from the sideline, is that the speaker did not mean to be humorous.

Interior Secretary Bruce Babbitt was one of several eulogists at Barry Goldwater's funeral. His exact words were not written down here, so they must be paraphrased. But the reaction was duly noted.

"There are two Arizona names recognized in every corner of this planet," said the former governor of the state, "and they are Barry Goldwater and Geronimo."

There was laughter from the thousands in the Tempe hall.

"Both had passionate love for the lands of Arizona," said Secretary Babbitt. Again laughter, but this time more of an uncertain titter.

"And both had a fierce and abiding passion for freedom." No laughter. The titterers finally got the point.

Perhaps the linkage wasn't so far-fetched. Perhaps Mr. Goldwater and Geronimo, the Chiricahua Apache chief, had much in common. Both were fierce, and both were driven, even though they fought to defend their chosen land in different times with different weapons.

• • •

The name of Geronimo has come to epitomize savagery. Gen. Nelson Miles described him as "the worst Indian who ever lived." He was seen by most historians as cunning and cruel, and he did more to resist the white man, whom he considered an invader, than any other. And yet you might wonder that if Mr. Goldwater were in Geronimo's moccasins, in those times, those cultures, under those terrible circumstances, would he (or many of us) have reacted differently.

Geronimo was a name given by the Spanish. His square name was Goyathay, meaning He-Who-Yawns in the

Chiricahua tongue. According to studies of Paul Wellman, Clark Wissler and others, Geronimo was a carefree, happy young buck who was admitted into the circle of warriors at 17, married an Apache maiden named Alope and fathered three children.

His tribe was at peace with the Mexican territory of Chihuahua. While the warriors were on a trading trip, the governor of neighboring Sonora, a bloodthirsty thief named Gen. Carasco, sent soldiers into the Apache camp. Scores of Indians, mostly women and children, were slaughtered, and nearly 100 were captured and sold into slavery in Mexico.

Geronimo returned from his trip to find his mother, wife and three children butchered. He later told interviewers, "I hardly knew what to do. I had no weapon, nor did I hardly wish to fight. I did not pray nor did I resolve to do anything in particular, for I had no purpose left." He returned to Arizona in silence; it was said that his lips thinned and curved down in a malevolent arc and that he never smiled again. But, goodness, how he fought.

• • •

Geronimo and his ragged band were starved into capture several times and moved from his beloved Arizona onto strange barren "reservations." He kept escaping the white man's bonds and fighting back savagely and conscienceless against any world that wasn't Apache.

As Mr. Wellman said, "In the name of 'civilization,' the white man shot down defenseless men, women and children at places like Camp Grant, Sand Creek and Wounded Knee, fed strychnine to Indian warriors, set whole villages of people out naked to freeze in the Montana winter and confined thousands in what amounted to concentration camps."

Years later, President John Kennedy wrote for *American Heritage,* "Our treatment of Indians during that period still affects the national conscience." That seems about as mildly as you could put it.

Eventually, Geronimo was taken in chains to a Florida

camp, later to Fort Sill and forever banned from his native Arizona territory. He was kept on a reservation as a prisoner of war. Tourists came to stare at him like a freak on the midway. He charged them 10 cents to pose for a hand-held camera, 25 cents for a tripod. He used the pittance to buy the white man's whiskey.

Mr. Goldwater was buried with pomp and circumstance and praise and 21-gun salutes. Geronimo, on a freezing February night in 1906, fell into an Oklahoma ditch and died of pneumonia. It doesn't take much imagination to see them both, as Secretary Babbitt hinted, as Arizona freedom fighters.

Jim Murray Earned a Respect Few Writers Achieve

(*Dallas Morning News,* August 20, 1998)

This was four hours after the World Series Earthquake of 1989, and reporters were scrambling madly in search of telephones that worked.

Writers had taken lap computers out of dark pressrooms into the gray passageways of Candlestick Park. But guards chased them from the premises in the gathering darkness, warning that the whole structure might collapse on their innocent brows.

One quartet of wretches somehow found the rental car on a dark lot and joined the frantic traffic down the Bay coast. Dan Foster drove, having somehow reached his Greenville, S.C., *News* before stadium phones went dead. The car's dome light glowed so the passengers could continue working the laptops.

Mr. Foster wheeled into several towns along the coastal highway where he saw flickering lights, but there, too, phone lines were kaput. Finally, off to the starboard, he spied a lighted gas station, and, lo, there was an outside phone booth with a live line.

Ed Pope's Eastern time zone deadline awarded him priority, so he took the first shift, balancing laptop on a lifted knee and reading his deathless prose to a note taker at the *Miami Herald.*

Finished, he relinquished the booth to Jim Murray to dictate his words to the *Los Angeles Times.*

As Mr. Pope left the booth, he saw a group of bikers nearby, glaring in his direction. They wore black leather, of course, and swollen biceps and tattoos and beards and caps and fierce eyes. They also wished to make telephone contact to the outside world, and as the booth continued to be occupied, their mutters increased and their glares intensified.

Finally, one large, greasy chap, obviously leader of the

pack, gestured firmly at the waiting Mr. Pope. The Miami columnist sighed; his time had come. His head was about to depart his body. He walked to the biker, who was again staring at the occupied booth. When he turned to Mr. Pope, his expression had softened considerably. Perhaps he was only going to tear off an arm or an ear.

"Tell me," he said almost reverently, "is that JIM MURRAY in there?"

· · ·

At a sports panel last month in Richmond, I told the earthquake story to younger newsmen to illustrate the Murray esteem. Jim was also a panelist, and he sloughed it off and quickly changed the subject. It was a typical reaction. He was not impressed with anyone and, most of all, himself.

That was one trait that made Mr. Murray unique in this time of inflated media egos. The headliners he wrote about were in awe of him, not the reverse. In 1984, when Bobby Knight bossed the U.S. Olympic basketballers, Mr. Murray wrote a column about the bombastic coach that was not entirely complimentary. Mr. Knight had the column enlarged and asked the author to autograph same. That, babies, is respect.

Of course, some never considered Jim Murray a sportswriter. Rather, we thought him an excellent, clever, imaginative writer who just happened to have sports as a subject. If you doubted his scope, try a conversation about opera, about the Russian novelists, about poetry from Oscar Wilde to Chic Sales, about the proper ratio of a martini or about how many elephants carried Hannibal across the Alps.

There were health problems you don't even want to know about. A pig valve in his heart. Blindness in one eye, partial sight in the other. A son lost to a drug overdose, a wife in a coma for a year.

He never complained, but we didn't sing "Galway Bay," his favorite song, at midnight there for a while. But then his second wife, Linda McCoy, revitalized his life for the last dozen years.

37

We have an annual visit, a half-dozen old cronies, and this spring at Phoenix, Jim seemed a bit pale and frail, and we made him quit after nine holes one day. But he laughed at the same old stories while he chugged on his nonalcoholic beer.

It was no great surprise when the call came Monday. But the thought persists as the plaudits around the country sing of his talent, his genuineness, thoughtfulness and humor. You might never guess, considering his physical ailments and his frailty, he was the toughest son-of-a-gun I've ever known.

Uncle Dick Was a Fighter Until the End

(Dallas Morning News, April 1, 1999)

His stock was Welsh-Irish, and he looked it. Square frame, square neck, square hands and fingers. He never would mention it, but family members spoke of genes tracing back to the Tennessee cavalry and how he made the arduous trip west under the canvas of his parents' wagon.

He had the stolid stubbornness of a farmer and, like blackland farmers of those days, spent daylight hours in blistering cotton fields, a sack of fried pork and corn pone and maybe a pickle and a burlap-wrapped jug of well water in the sparse shade of flanking bushes.

Everyone called him Uncle Dick and respected his strength and kindness. He laughed a bit in those days and, at Saturday night gatherings, played the fiddle for the younguns. On Sundays, he put on a stiff collar and took his family to the country church, which he had helped build.

And after a shared noon meal with other families—fried chicken, potato salad, stewed carrots, corn and mince pie, brought and spread by womenfolk on board tables under shade trees—he opened a wooden bin inside the church and removed baseball gear for a game in a scruffy flanking field.

And at daylight Monday, he would be back in the fields, fighting an invasion of Johnson grass and boll weevil and frequently, hopelessly, sweeping the sky in desperate search of rain clouds.

When depression struck and cotton prices plunged, his crops rotted in the field, not worth picking and hauling to the gin, and like so many neighbors, he lost the farm and a big part of himself. His hair was white before he turned 40.

• • •

He moved his small family to a country hamlet, put away the fiddle and sent away precious dollars for four instruction books on carpentry, sturdy black volumes with spines of red leather, filled with mysterious hieroglyphics and stiff technical wordage.

Goodness, how he studied those books, learning how to sink foundations, fit studs and joists and rafters, fashion saw-jacks and ladders, mix cement with a hoe in a wheelbarrow for brick fireplaces and chimneys. Paint, paper, plaster, lay hardwood floor and linoleum, connect pipes, whatever.

He built everything in the little town: houses, barns, garages and sheds. He replaced roofs and remodeled old homes. Name it, Uncle Dick built it.

His life was work, work, work. No precious moments were squandered on idle conversation, the battery radio or dominoes. All the whiskey he ever drank in his life, he once said, wouldn't fill a fruit jar.

Work was his narcotic, work until sunset, then a tub bath and supper and a chair under the floor lamp, a sack of Bull Durham and a book, any book, even dime pulps like *Wild West Weekly* and *Ranch Romances*. Early to bed and awake, automatically, at dawn. There wasn't an alarm clock in the house.

• • •

Well into his 70s, he climbed ladders, pounded 10-penny nails and sawed two-by-fours. After that, he couldn't take it easy. He built desks, chests, bookshelves and coffee tables as gifts for kinsmen. He was still at it when the stroke took away movement in both legs and an arm.

Then he spent three years in a hospital bed set up in his daughter's spare bedroom, never complaining, speaking when spoken to, puffing his "ready rolls" and staring at the somber wallpaper. One could only guess at the depth of his despair, especially when the practical nurse bathed and shaved him, combed his white hair and attended to the personal hygiene of this once independent man.

Uncle Dick so passed his 91st birthday, silent and helplessly scourged to his dungeon. And had there, perchance, come a knock on the front door and there stood Dr. Jack

Kevorkian, we would have baked him a cake, and my grandfather, could he have managed, would have crawled to the grocery to fetch the flour and eggs.

The Days of Titanic Hustles

(*Dallas Morning News,* November 4, 1999)

Perhaps, at long last, they're going to do a movie about Titanic Thompson. Seems to memory, it has been in the works for a lifetime or so, snagged in those mysterious labyrinths that often beset film projects.

Now, the golfer Gary McCord and the producer Ron Shelton (*Bull Durham* and *Tin Cup*) say they have a done deal with Disney for a film based on Titanic Thompson, who died in 1978 in a Fort Worth nursing home. Cosner is interested, they say. Eastwood is interested. Blah blah blah.

The tide is running out on Titanic. Already, there are few remaining who trade stories about the old hustler, some true, some fictional. Such as:

After winning a bet on the skeet range, Titanic taunts his victim, the club champ: "Why, you're not much shot at all. I'll bet you $10,000 my wife can beat you." (Unbeknownst to the sucker, Titanic was married to a national skeet champ.)

Or: "Why, you're no fun. I'll double the bet and play you left-handed. (Unbeknownst to the mark, Titanic was a natural southpaw.)

• • •

Years ago, the sportswriter Oscar Fraley attempted to collaborate on a Thompson book. He quit after a couple of sessions. We talked about it later, after Thompson relatives had contacted me (among others) about reviving the project. "He didn't want to tell the truth about everything," said Mr. Fraley. "He just wanted to repeat the old stories."

The writer was especially interested in whether Titanic, as rumored, sat in on that mysterious poker game in the Park Central Hotel when gambler Arnold Rothstein was shot. Titanic resented the accusation and the court appearance that followed, for they made him famous. It was said that Damon

Runyon based his character Sky Masterson in *Guys and Dolls* on Titanic, and it blew his cover.

He much preferred to be the tall, quiet, nameless bystander who would shoot pool with you, play cards, pitch horseshoes, shoot skeet, shoot pistols, play golf or bowl. Name it, he would play it for a price, under conditions that always seemed to favor Titanic, for such is the hustler's creed.

And the worst thing that can happen for a hustler is to become famous.

• • •

During his later years, Titanic lived in the Village Apartments here and hustled around the little nine-hole course there. He also hung out at the Cotton Bowling Palace on Lemmon Avenue, bowling, shooting pool and betting a sucker he could throw a door key in the keyhole three out of five times (he could) or sail a playing card across the lounge, through the serving slot into the kitchen (he could).

I heard a rare story from Curtis Sanford, owner of the Bowling Palace.

One afternoon, a young corporal from Fort Hood showed up at the pool tables, flashed a fat roll of bills, played a sharp game of pool against the regulars and brashly challenged the house. Titanic watched in silence.

"You shoot a pretty good stick," Ty finally said. "You play any other games?"

"Well," said the kid, who apparently didn't know Titanic from Adam. "I play a little gin."

"Got any money?"

"You bet. I got my mustering-out pay from the Army and several thousand more from barracks games."

A dozen bystanders nudged each other. This is classic. Old Ty is setting him up. The smart aleck kid is fixing to learn something.

The party adjourned to a nearby apartment. Titanic put up three thousand, and the eager hangers on, all backing Titanic, dug deep for another ten gees. The cocky youngster covered all bets.

To everyone's stunning surprise, the GI turned out to be an excellent gin player. The game was close, but he edged the old hustler, collected all the bets and left.

Then, unbeknownst to the crowd, the youth and Ty met the next day, split the winnings, returned the soldier suit to the costume rental shop and went on their separate, merry and larcenous ways.

No Peanuts, No Pogo—Woe Are We

(Dallas Morning News, January 6, 2000)

Oh, well, it could be of some comfort that I picked up another two minutes a day to spend on whatever strikes my jaded fancy. At a certain age, those two minutes come in 24-karat gold and deserve a place on the mantelpiece or perhaps in the family safe.

Charles Schulz, because of health problems, is retiring his Peanuts comic strip of 50 years, and therefore, the time devoted daily to the wisdom of Charlie Brown and his pals may be employed elsewhere.

Some years ago, there came the feeling that comic strips weren't comic anymore and that I could save 15 minutes in a more educational pursuit, such as found in the Racing Form. Except, that is, for Peanuts and Pogo, two stubborn bastions of humor against invasions by Mary Worth and Judge Parker and all their serious problems.

• • •

A century or so ago, we all were comic-strip addicts. Maggie giving Jiggs what-for for bringing home a pail of corned beef and cabbage from the neighborhood bar. Hans and Fritz, the Katzenjammer Kids, tormenting the Captain. Barney Google and his racehorse Sparkplug in various hustles. Major Hoople astounding boardinghouse cronies with various falsehoods. Hillbilly Snuffy Smith and his moonshine jug marked XXX.

And, of course, there was Dagwood, trying to nap on the sofa when he wasn't embarrassing wife Blondie, son Alexander and boss Mr. Dithers with some sort of stupidity.

Somewhere along the line, the comic page became less comic and more soap operatic, or at least it seemed to us traditionalists.

The retirement of Mr. Schulz this week is a blow topped only by the death of Walt Kelly in 1973 after a quarter-century of the delightful doings of Pogo, the genial possum and his pals in the Okeefenokee Swamp—Albert, the cigar-smoking alligator; Mam'selle Hepzibah, the demure French skunk; Churchy Lafemme, the philosophical turtle; Wizard, the professional dog; and any number of other regulars. (One character was Dr. Howland Owl, a nearsighted scientist intent on inventing "the Adam bomb." Another, a speechmaking pig, bore a marked resemblance to Nikita Khrushchev.)

To term Walt Kelly a comic-strip artist is to call Mrs. Carlo Ponti a female. To this mind anyway, he was a full-throated genius, a humorist and satirist and philosopher of awesome depth. He did satires on Russian novels (*War Nor Peace*), fairy tales (*Goldie Lox and the Fore Bares*) and even Christmas carols, like the immortal:

Deck us all with Boston Charlie
Walla Walla Wash an' Kalamazoo
Nora's freezin' on the trolley
Swaller dollar cauliflower Alley-ga-roo.

Often, you had to dip deep beneath the dialogue for the prime meat. I remember a road trip with the old Fort Worth Cats baseball team when some of us lingered over breakfast in the railroad diner, laughing at the latest strip.

A second baseman named Spook Jacobs interrupted. "I can't read Pogo," he said glumly. "I only got a high school education."

• • •

Other than his newspaper strips, Mr. Kelly authored books of cartoon art and philosophy. They are all on my shelves, a dozen or so, read almost to tatters, shrines for frequent pilgrimages into hallowed halls of humor.

"Naturally, the humorist in any age is viewed with some misgivings, for he plays with no particular team," he once wrote. "So as we move along, we cannot care who sings our country's songs, beneath the high notes of patriotism, we want to hear the low notes of laughter, always off-key, always true."

Then there was his classic theft of Commodore Perry's

Lake Erie dispatch, when Mr. Kelly beseeched readers to stop taking life some grimly:

"Resolve then, that on this very ground, with small flags waving and tinny blasts on tiny trumpets, we shall meet the enemy. And not only may he be ours, he may be us."

Even if you never read another Kelly word, this was enough to make you join his forces.

Yule Tied

(*Dallas Morning News,* December 23, 1999)

Sometime, somewhere, I read that the bean counters say a newspaper's readership turns over every three years. Or maybe it was five years. Or maybe it was pea counters. At any rate, I swiped this plot from Red Smith and have written this story several times before, during the last quarter-century, on this and other newspapers. It is repeated here not because of laziness, although that ain't a bad reason, but simply because in the usually scruffy orbit of sports, it is the best Christmas story I know.

Billy Miske was a solid blue-collar boxer who always gave a dollar's worth. He fought Jack Dempsey three times, the last bout for the heavyweight title. It was back when you could knock a guy down and then stand over him and slug him when he tried to get up, like on a saloon parking lot. The brutal Mr. Dempsey did that to Mr. Miske for three rounds.

Billy also boxed Tommy Gibbons, Battling Levinski and Harry Greb, whose ma was frightened by a buzz saw. Twice, Mr. Miske went 10 rounds with Mr. Greb to no decisions. He was young, and, as they say, he was willing. He was no bum. He also was a dedicated husband and father.

When Billy was 25, he was stricken by a terrible fever. Doctors shook their heads sadly and advised him to quit the ring. But Billy didn't have a trade, and he had a family and bills. Boxing was the only work he knew, so he kept at it. In 1922, at the age of 28, he had 16 bouts.

Now, he was 29, and his kidneys were shot; he was dying of Bright's disease, but he told no one except his manager. He had one bout, early in January, and then for months he was too weak to go to the gymnasium. He stayed home with his wife and two children and tried to stretch his meager savings.

But now the calendar was coming up to Christmas 1923, and his wallet was flat.

In early November, Billy Miske left his bed of pain, dressed and went slowly downtown in Minneapolis to see his old friend and manager, Jack Reddy.

"Get me a fight," said Billy.

"You're not serious," said Mr. Reddy.

"I mean it," Mr. Miske said grimly. "I got to have just one more fight."

The manager was Billy's only confidant, and he kept shaking his head until the fighter said, "Listen to me. I'm busted. I can't afford a single Christmas gift for my family. I won't be around next year, and I'd like to have my family around me, all happy, for just one more Christmas."

"I don't like to say this," said the manager, "but if you went in the ring now, in your condition, you might be killed."

Billy Miske shrugged. "What's the difference?" he said.

The manager squirmed. "Well, do this for me," he said. "Go to the gym and start working, and let's see if you can get into some kind of shape. Then, we'll talk."

"That's out," said the boxer. "You know I can't work. I can't get in shape, but I got to have this one more fight."

Jack Reddy finally surrendered. He matched Billy with Bill Brennan in Omaha. Mr. Brennan also had fought Jack Dempsey and had gone 12 rounds. He was downhill, but he still was big, rough, dangerous and honest.

Mr. Miske didn't go near the gym. He stayed home, swallowed soup and aspirin and tried to conserve his strength until it was time for him and his manager to board the train for Omaha.

After the fight, the pale, spent Billy Miske picked up his $2,400 purse, went back to Minneapolis and blew the bundle on presents. It was the grandest Christmas ever in the Miske household. There was a feast and music and laughter and piles of gifts, and Mr. and Mrs. Billy Miske and their two children were together and gloriously happy.

・ ・ ・

On December 26, Mr. Miske rang Jack Reddy. "Come take me to the hospital," he said calmly, "I'm dying."

And on New Year's Day 1924, in a St. Paul hospital, quietly and with dignity, Billy Miske died.

The Omaha fight had been six weeks before, and his friends, when the story came out, couldn't believe it. Billy was weak and dying, and it would have made sense for him to fake a quick knockout, take the count, grab his money and run. But he didn't. Billy Miske knocked out Bill Brennan in four rounds. You could look it up.

A Legend in His Own Mind

D, The Magazine of Dallas (1970)

"Mr. Jack Proctor, to hear him spell it, sailed the seven seas, wrestled professionally, captured John Dillinger single-handedly, taught Will Rogers how to chew gum, and invented the sand wedge."

The way he told it, Jack Proctor awoke one noon in his sleazy garage apartment in Cleburne, Texas, and dismally considered whether he was alive or dead. Except for the pulsating pain in his head, Proctor was numb and he concluded from dreary experience that feeling would soon creep back into his extremities, accompanied by excruciating jeebies. This was a traumatic stage whenever Jack Proctor sobered up, which was not at all often.

To compound his miseries, the courthouse clock on the nearby Johnson County courthouse started banging its noon message—torture beyond justification for a man in Proctor's state. Ten bongs, eleven bongs, twelve bongs, thirteen—*what?* Fourteen, fifteen. The clangs came more rapidly until they were almost a single heinous note.

He could see the clock from his only window and when he got his aching eyes in focus, he saw the hands spinning on the huge clock face. He knew this was it. He had finally flipped. Oceans of rum and cheap gin and foul scotch and raw bourbon, over two decades, had done it. He was not yet dead; he was bound in alcoholic purgatory. There, with the hideous vibrations beating against his poor skull and the giant hands circling the dial, Proctor promised the Lord and whoever else was listening that, given a pass from this horrible joint, he would never put another demon drop down his neck.

It wasn't until days later Jack discovered that workmen were repairing the courthouse clock that day and that the hands really *were* spinning and the bongs bonging. But he had made his pact and in his remaining 18 years, Proctor never broke it.

(Of course, he did get onto some suspicious cough drops later on. They were Vicks, he said, but were made with such a strong narcotic ingredient that he had to buy them in a liquor store.)

You could put the lie to the cough drops—although he *did* seem to use an uncommon lot—but the courthouse narrative *might* have been valid. But when you started separating the truths from the untruths, you destroyed the person.

I once wrote in a 1965 *Dallas Times Herald* column: "Mr. Jack Proctor, before he became editor of *The Richardson Daily News,* led a most adventurous life to hear him spell it. He sailed the seven seas, wrestled professionally under the name of Jim Londos, captured John Dillinger single-handedly while posing as a broad in a red dress. He frequently dated Norma Shearer, taught Will Rogers how to chew gum and invented the sand wedge. This is not to say Mr. Jack Proctor takes liberty with the truth. It is hard indeed to take liberty with a stranger. Chances are Mr. Jack Proctor wouldn't recognize the truth if it walked into his bedroom, sat on his chest and fed him oatmeal with a great horn spoon."

Minutes after these words appeared on the street, Jack Proctor called to say his lawyer would be in touch shortly with notice of a libel suit, but in the meantime how about meeting at Shanghai Jimmy's for some chili and rice.

It was in Cleburne, Texas, in 1947, that I joined the Proctor cult. He was in Cleburne out of necessity. The *Times-Review* was desperate for a sportswriter-newsman, and Proctor was desperate for a job of any sort. He had been fired off a half-dozen sheets because of the bottle and he departed his last stop, Galveston, rather hurriedly because he also had hung paper—meaning he had written several checks that were not immediately, and never would be, negotiable.

Cleburne was a good hideout for him. It was in a dry county, but was only an hour's bus ride from the nearest liquor store in Fort Worth. Every payday, Proctor would put on his overcoat, no matter the temperature, and catch the Greyhound for Cowtown, where he would fill his many pockets with half-pints. This is the mark of a drunk, he later explained. Half-pints are handy to carry without making a telltale bulge; you are never without help.

First time I remember seeing Proctor was at a high school bi-district football game in Cleburne. There was this small, dapper guy in his early forties, with a pencil moustache and big brown bird dog eyeballs and roached brown hair, chain-smoking and gabbing. I tabbed him for a pro juicer because a real hooked boozer never wants to drink in front of witnesses if he can avoid it. He ain't proud of it.

Almost everybody in pressboxes in those days carried a little stimulant, partly to negate the cold wind that came through the cracks, partly because they thought it made them more fluid and lucid at the typewriter, and partly because they had seen *The Front Page* too many times. Proctor had nothing showing. No tattletale bulge. He would disappear from the ramshackle pressbox occasionally, and when he returned his eyes would be brighter, he would smoke more feverishly and jabber louder and faster. I was on *The Fort Worth Press* at the time, and Proctor read our paper daily, he said, and was familiar with some of the crap we were trying. He also said, at great length while I was trying to watch the Bryans or the Corsicanas or the Temples or whoever the hell was bidistricting, that he had once managed Fritzie Zivic and had promoted fights on the Gulf Coast and had worked on all the old Dallas papers during The Good Old Newspaper Days and was on first-name basis with every broke and shill and asspocket bookie and whorelady on Galveston Island and why didn't I come visit him at Cleburne sometime.

The next I heard from Jack Proctor, a dowdy little woman in a flowery bonnet walked in the *Press* office, said she had ridden a train from Cleburne and did I know where Jack Proctor could be found, as they had been married a couple nights ago and seems like he had since disappeared. No, it wasn't a regular wedding, she said. She thought he called it a

53

Scottish Rite ceremony and that, somehow, she suspected I had spirited Jack Proctor away from her side.

Well, Proctor always denied the story but it did not escape nor ease my discomfort at the moment, especially because I excused myself to go to the men's room and stayed there two hours until the poor woman despaired of my returning and left.

Along about then, Proctor was going through the legend of the bonging courthouse clock and swore off. He joined Alcoholics Anonymous and became an energetic worker in same, although it never seemed to bother him to be among the rest of us degenerates when we were popping tops or choking down cheap bourbon.

Jack became a LaGrave Field pressbox regular, when Bobby Bragan's Cats were at home, and he soon became the non-resident elder statesman and historian and constant lecturer to the *Press* sports staff, a rather unorthodox collection that included Dan Jenkins, Bud Shrake, Jerre Todd, Charley Modessette, Puss Ervin, Andy Anderson, Gary Cartwright and others who came and went with lesser ripples. Proctor recognized no one, however, by his proper handle. Sherrod became Blackwood Sheridan. Jenkins was Jenke, Shrake was Thor because he was nine feet tall. Todd was Spanky, The Child Star; Modesette was, naturally enough, Modesty; and Anderson was Andrews. Then Proctor had a few Cleburne pals whom he inducted into the group, a *Times-Review* reporter named Pete Smith whom Proctor called Puck Smythe and a giant Yellow Page salesman he referred to as Bad Hair Bentley, obviously because of a flat mat of red brillo on his head. Proctor, for some reason, renamed himself Saintly Julien. It seemed to fit as well as anything else.

There also were other Cleburnites named Mad Adam and Ugly and Emit Mewhinney and a black man who worked at a gas station whom Proctor called Yere-Yee.

What?

"A black has a special tuning fork in his ear, like a dog, that can hear sounds nobody else can," Proctor explained seriously.

"Yere-yee is one of those sounds. Look, I'll show you." This first happened when we were standing on Akard Street in downtown Dallas. Across on the other side, forty yards away, a black man walked in the opposite direction.

Jack put his hand to his mouth. "Yere-yee!" he shouted. Sure enough, the black man wheeled in his tracks and looked back at us.

"See?" said Proctor, quite satisfied with himself. Of course, *other* pedestrians and a couple truck drivers also turned and looked at us, a fact Proctor blithely ignored.

Proctor loved Afro-Americans. Once we were in a buffet line at a press luncheon in the Fort Worth Club. An old black man was ladling the barbecued shrimp, a dish dearly loved by Proctor. While standing in line, Jack devised a way to get an extra large helping.

"Watch me bring him," he whispered. "Watch me give him some numbers talk," referring to the ghetto policy racket.

Proctor reached the shrimp cauldron and held out his plate.

"Fo, lebben and forty-fo," Jack said.

The old man did not even glance up. "Straight up and down," he said automatically. "Thas the Dixie Queen."

Then he lifted his eyes for the first time and stared at Proctor, who was grinning.

"I'd say you have been among my people," the old man said.

"Born in Memphis," Jack said.

"Well, I admit, on Beale Street," said the old man, "one do occasionally see a colored face." Then he heaped shrimp on Proctor's plate until his thumbs were buried.

Proctor had his own language. State cops were highway petroleums; the guy with the drill was a tooth dentist. Women of the streets were whoreladies. Then there was his backwards gimmick. Tattoo was too-tatt. Jail was gowhoose. A big car, regardless of the make, was a Cadillac-Buick. And when he called on the telephone, there never would be a hello. He would start the conversation in the middle.

55

"*Times Herald* sports—Sherrod."

"He ought to be walking in the door now."

"Who, for crissakes, who ought to be walking in the door?"

"The lawyer. He has the libel papers to serve you. I don't stand still for no watermelon conversation like you strapped on me in today's paper."

"Bite me."

"This is chili-and-rice day. Meet you at Shanghai Jimmy's at twelve-thirty." Click.

You eventually got used to his telephone style. It was a challenge.

"*Times Herald* sports."

"His last name was Doss."

There would be a silence while I would fight the clue frantically. It was a disgrace to show confusion. Finally a cog would catch.

"First name, Noble," I'd say. "From Temple, Texas."

"He caught the pass that beat A&R, right?" (For some reason, it was always Texas A&R with Proctor. Or TCR. Or SMR.)

"Right."

"Later." Click.

Once the two of us were at a Fort Worth baseball game, looking over the pressbox rail, when we saw a drunk defy gravity. He was weaving up the aisle, trying to find his row, when he stumbled on a step. Like an invisible wire was jerking him, he fell this way and that, but always upward, until he finally plopped flat on his can some ten rows above his destination.

"Man and boy," said Proctor. "I see drunks fall for forty years. I see drunks fall off bar stools, off curbs and docks, out of windows and cars and trees. This," he said, "is the first time I ever see one fall upstairs."

He never forgot this marvel; he filed it away with an unending supply of other marvels gathered in his newspaper lifetime. Conversation never dragged when Proctor was in the huddle, for he would pull out one of his memories and weave it in the most fascinating style. Unfortunately, he couldn't put

56

it down at the typewriter, but he talked a mean game. (We were all great Damon Runyon fans at the time, and Proctor walked straight from the pages.)

There was a one-eyed cowpoke Proctor once knew who ate the same breakfast every morning in a café at Iraan, Texas: flapjacks, chili on the side and a bottle of Pearl. There was the old Dallas police reporter who was beset with the idea of killing himself and tried it often when he was juiced up. One morning, the reporter showed up for work at the police press-room with a Band-Aid on his forehead. He had tried to shoot himself and missed. The others laughed and laughed to see such sport.

"You're right," the guy said morosely, "I coulda done more damage with a rock."

And then there was the Cleburne middleweight, Jack Something, whom Proctor managed. Had to scratch his tiger from a Fort Worth Golden Gloves bout because the fighter had taken a fearful beating from his older brother the night before.

"He stole a horse and brought it home, the idiot," Proctor grumbled.

"Well, his brother was trying to teach him a lesson," somebody said.

"Oh, he didn't whip him for *that,*" said Proctor. "He whipped him for not stealing the saddle, too."

Proctor's favorite local character—perhaps he was fiction too—was named Fate Callahan and he was a moonshiner from Goat Neck, a small community near Cleburne.

"They tell me Fate makes the best stuff in these parts," said Jack, now very much the towteedler. "Fate tells me he started that famous guessing game."

That famous guessing game?

"Three guys come out to Fate's house and buy a quart of his shine, then go into the front room and drink it. One would go to the can and the other two try to guess which one left."

Proctor's yarns were tricky; as fanciful as they sounded, you dassn't challenge.

He had a faded tootatt on his left arm. An eagle, I think it

Incredible People

was, with the word "Trixie" underneath. For years he had told of a Kansas City spree during which he and his fiancée of the moment got soused and wound up on skid row, where they got tattooed with each other's names. We all scoffed. One night, during a Cotton Bowl week in Dallas, Jack called me to his room in the old Jefferson Hotel. He introduced me to a strawhaired biddy of considerable vintage. He said, meet Trixie, an old girlfriend from Kansas City.

I stared hard at him. He looked back blandly, but squarely.

"Excuse me, ma'am," I said, a little triumphantly, "this guy..."

Jack interrupted. "Show him," he said.

The old gal obediently raised her skirt above one plump knee. There was a tattoo: J*A*C*K. Proctor turned to gaze at the window. I could see his shoulders shaking.

Jack worked the Dallas police beat for the *Dispatch* back during the mid-30s, when the city abounded with legendary newshounds like Ira Wellborn; Eddie Barr, one of Proctor's occasional brothers-in-law; Red Webster; a sports editor who called himself The Great Ben Hill, who ran a horsebook out of his lower right-hand desk drawer; a gal named Soapy Suggs; a telegraph editor named Wilbur Shaw who—Proctor vowed—would drink ten pints of gin in process of a day's editions. And there were many others—the dour wit Ken Hand, Lewis Bailey, Bill Duncan, Marihelen MacDuff, Frank Harting, Pat Kleinman, Clarke Newlon, Flint D. Dupre, Pierce McBride, Willie Ward, Mabel Duke—whom our particular clique knew only through Proctor's outbursts of fact and fantasy.

These, I suppose, were The Good Old Newspaper Days. There were four Dallas newspapers, all fiercely competitive; bootleg gin was a dollar a pint, delivered; hookers were a deuce; there was a place named the State Café where owners would let reporters eat on the tab until payday. And the Texas Centennial celebration in 1936 had brought all sorts of interesting imports into town. Some, Proctor hinted darkly, were from Chicago and wore black suits and hats all the time.

"Listen, if the police reporter didn't come up with an exclusive every day, or a new angle every edition, the city editor might fire him on the spot," Proctor recalled. "Police stories sold the newspapers. If there wasn't a story, we made 'em up."

Jim Chambers, now chairman of the *Times Herald*, remembers one slow news day when Proctor and other cop shop authors were desperate for a story. Proctor went outside for a walk, and noticed police property men dumping confiscated bootleg whiskey on the curb. It was running in a rivulet down the sloped gutter, underneath parked cars. He looked both ways, tossed a lighted match into the stream and raced to the telephone with FIERY HOLOCAUST SWEEPS COMMERCE STREET. The fire destroyed three cars.

"I knew more about Dallas than any living citizen," Proctor bragged. "Why, when a fire was reported, the truck man would call me and ask directions. 'Twenty-two hundred York,' the guy would say, and I'd say, 'turn off at Calmont, up four blocks, yellow house on the left with a bore dark tree in the yard and watch out for the dog.'"

Proctor once had a girlfriend in San Antonio, so he convinced his city editor (it could have been at any of the four papers, since he worked on all at various times) that he had set up an exclusive, private interview with Clyde Barrow at a certain hour at a certain farmhouse near San Antonio. The editor drooled. Barrow was the country's leading mad dog. So Proctor was sent to San Antonio and wrote a daring, graphic account of his personal chat with the criminal, his pleas for understanding, a story resplendent in detail and description, the kerosene lamp light flickering on the gaunt planes of the killer's face and so on. Hot damn.

Proctor returned to his Dallas office, confident of backslaps and maybe even a bonus. Instead, the city editor was loud and furious when he instructed Proctor to get the hell out and never come back. It seems at the exact same time Proctor was interviewing Barrow in that farmhouse, so glowingly described in Jack's fictitious yarn, Barrow was positively placed 250 miles north, busily putting a shotgun charge in a highway petroleum.

Bingo Joe Luther, an old-time friend from the sheriff's force, and Ken Hand and Red Webster and Jim Chambers would spill similar Proctor stories and he would laugh along with the rest when the tales were relayed, but would never admit to any belief that he was not history's greatest legman.

Proctor would tell of his ever-loving wife, first of many, who was one of the prettiest and no worse than a show bet in the mean department. Shot him five times in the head with a .32 revolver, he said. "Never missed me a time," Proctor would say proudly. Then he would doff his snap-brim hat, part his brown hair and show you the scars. Or, show you *some* scars.

Bingo Joe Luther told about the time Proctor went on a midnight dice game raid in a rundown area with the vice squad. He was standing on the front porch, dark as pitch, when the cops flushed the game. A woman brushed by Proctor, and he felt a slight sting across the stomach.

"What he really hated," said Bingo Joe, "is he had on this brand-new suit some gambler had laid on him. This gal and her razor made him look like Emmett Kelley."

Proctor said he chased the whorelady, caught her when she crawled under a culvert and kicked her in the puss a couple times and then went to City Emergency hospital for a patch job. Holding a towel to his stomach while the doc threaded the needle, he called his ever-loving.

"Honey, I'm at the . . ." he began.

"Listen, you bastard, do you know what time it is?"

"Well, I know, but I've been cut and I'm at the hospital..."

"I don't care where you are or what you've done! How many times have I told you don't *never* wake me up at this hour of the morning!"

Proctor was married, near as he could count, seven times. But he said it actually amounted to five because he married a couple of them twice.

He married a nice widow lady in Cleburne—refined, religious, rather well-to-do. Jack was the most entertaining person ever in her sheltered life. Heck, Proctor went respectable.

They built a $65,000 home on the outskirts of Cleburne, with a trickling creek running through the backyard; he filled huge closets with fancy sports shirts and jackets, bought a cockatoo named Norton and a Weimaraner pup which, of course, he called a wisenhammer.

The dog, Impervious, was a prodigy. Proctor complained that he often had to stay up late, reading Homer and Socrates to his pet. "If I try to read him *The Fort Worth Press,* he bites me," said Saintly Julien. "Especially the sports section."

The neighbors complained. "Impervious goes down to the creek and catches all the perch, brings them back, cleans and puts them in the freezer. The neighbor kids don't like it."

To contain Impervious, Proctor had a six-foot chain fence built around the backyard.

"First day, he cleared it in a single jump," Jack reported. "Went to the creek and brought back a batch of shrimp."

Shrimp?

"Fresh water shrimp," he said. "Delicacy of Johnson County."

Proctor said he raised the fence to seven feet.

"He jumped it the first try. I got to go to eight."

The next day. "Well, he jumped that one, too. The Mexican yard guys say they can't go any higher. Something about Civil Aeronautic regulations. But I'll think of something."

Months later. "What did you ever do about Impervious?"

"I cut off one of his legs."

"That do it?"

"Naw. Damn thing grew back."

This particular Mrs. Proctor owned an auto supply house and a Nash distributorship. Moonlighting from his Cleburne newspaper job, Jack sold cars. Sold a bunch.

"Safest car ever built," he would say, slamming his hand on the fender. "I can show you government reports. During the last calendar year, only two people were killed in a Nash automobile. And they were both bank robbers, shot at a roadblock."

Bill Rives, then the sports editor of the *Dallas News,*

bought a Nash. So did a couple other newspapermen. Hell, I bought two, one a little Metropolitan made in England. I wondered about gasoline mileage.

"Gas!" Proctor roared. "Whoever told you this car uses gas? It *makes* gas. Once a week, you gotta drain out a gallon or two or it'll flood on you."

Once, the lady of our house, who also had bought a Nash from Proctor, used a fancy Ambassador demonstrator on a loan arrangement and apologized when she returned the car because it was almost out of gas.

"Oh, thank goodness you didn't put any gasoline in this machine," said Proctor, wiping his forehead in relief. "I forgot to tell you. This car runs on frankincense and myrrh."

Once he was late for a dinner party at our house.

"I keep forgetting how powerful this Ambassador is," he told the guests. "I had to stop and have two Cadillac-Buicks removed from my tailpipe."

That marriage dissolved also, then Jack wed what he called a "runner." Occasionally when he'd come home from work, she would have run off. Next was Betty, a ravishingly beautiful brunette whom Jack met through his work with the AAs.

About that time Proctor disappeared from the Southwest pressboxes for a couple of months. We would call and he was vague with his reasons. We thought probably he was recovering from a busted nose or something similar because people were always putting the slug on Proctor. Once, a wealthy rancher named Sexton died and there was a big hullabaloo over his will and Proctor covered the court proceedings like he was Heywood Broun at the Scopes trial. The *Times-Review* readership wasn't accustomed to this Front Page Farrell type of reporting, so Sexton's ranch foreman occasionally looked up Jack and gave him a black eye.

Proctor once covered a high school game in which the referee, as he was giving the signal about which team won the toss, was seized with a cramp in his leg and fell to the ground, writhing in pain. The umpire bent over to administer at the instant the referee desperately kicked his foot in an effort to rid himself of this spasm. He kicked the umpire squarely in the mouth, knocking out a couple teeth. The umpire reeled blindly and fell over the Cisco team captain who had knelt to tie his shoe. The team captain suffered a broken collarbone. Proctor, in his game prose, referred to the officials as the Marx Brothers. The referee happened upon the editor on a Cleburne street the next week and whopped him on the eye. Proctor had always told his audience that he had both boxed and rassled professionally, but apparently the referee didn't know that, for he bopped Proctor several times on the eye. Suddenly, as fate ironically decreed, the referee was stricken with the same muscle spasm that had beset him in the game, and he fell to the sidewalk. Proctor then tried to kick the fallen man, but his vision was so blurred by his swollen eyes that he missed, and booted a nearby fireplug instead, breaking a toe.

Anyways, the reason Proctor was missing from the scene, we soon discovered, was that he had all his teeth pulled. When he did show, it was with a sparkling set of storeboughts.

"Fit?" he said. "You ask if they fit? Listen, this job is the marvel of the dental world. They're writing clinic papers on it. These teeth fit so well, they're actually growing into my gums. See this one?" he tapped an incisor, "I had to have the damn thing filled last week!"

For a half-dozen years, Proctor and his Cleburne cohorts sponsored what they called a Mid-Winter Olympics for the Press sports staff. It was an overnight affair, climaxing with a 100-yard dash at dawn which nobody, to my recollection, ever finished. Proctor made his plans in great secrecy, bidding us meet on a Cleburne hotel parking lot at midnight, then guiding the procession through the night to somebody's borrowed lake house or ranch house or, on one occasion, an abandoned motel.

Proctor, as Saintly Julien, always dressed in some outlandish costume, insisted that everybody prepare some sort of act to liven the proceedings. As the affair was stag, some of the acts would get a little raunchy. But some were quite artistic. Jenkins and Todd once wrote a complete musical, sang and

63

danced with strawhats and canes. Shrake, Sherrod and Cartwright once rehearsed a trapeze act called The Flying Huzars in which they appeared in long underwear and capes. Proctor wrote a play, a three-act drama entitled *Is This Then All?*, cast with his Cleburne chums, including Yere-Yee, and it was so bad it made your eyes water. Proctor turned his cap around backward, wore puttees, sat in a canvas chair and directed the thing through a megaphone. And then there was the indelible memory of Andy Anderson, old aviator's leather helmet on, goggles and all, lights out and only a flashlight shining up into his somber face as he sang a cappella, *Lucky Lindbergh, Hero of the U.S.A.*

One day, word trickled. Summertime, 1962. Proctor had a sore spot on his gum that wouldn't heal. Biopsy. The Big C. Some of us visited him at Harris Hospital in Fort Worth the night before the operation. He was sitting up in bed, telling of the *Dispatch* story he once wrote about a guy—now quite prominent in Las Vegas—who hit another on the head with a piece of his car. "Benny Binion, the Bumper Beater, I called him," said Jack. "Binion bought extra copies. Thought it was the greatest thing he ever read."

The operation lasted ten hours, and they took away part of his jaw and face. Hours later, in the intensive care unit, he was sprawled with tubes and pipes sticking out of his gray skin and gauze and tape covered his head and face except for one eye, peeping from the whole mess, flicking here and there wildly, like a trapped fawn. The eye swept across me, unrecognizing, I thought, until he made a feeble scratching motion with his right hand. A bedside nurse hurriedly put a pad under his hand and a pencil between his chalky fingers. She cranked his bed slightly and he slowly, laboriously scratched on the pad until finished. He fell back in his bandages, his one eye flickering past me to other restless points. I picked up the pad. In quivering, pitiful hieroglyphics were three words: Need poon tang.

Some of the newspaper wretches around the state pitched in their mites to help pay some of Jack's hospital expenses. His

Cleburne job, almost unbelievably, was not waiting for him when he got out of the hospital. Some other calls were made and Lorin McMullen put Jack to work on the *Fort Worth Star-Telegram* copy rim. Then he moved to a better post—editor of the *Richardson Daily News.* His visits and calls over the next couple years came a little less frequently, and his newspaper pals, those of us who were not too busy going our own ways, thought it was because of his scarred face—maybe he was awaiting some scheduled plastic surgery before he would again join the crowd. Because it was *his* crowd.

Who knows? Maybe the Big C wasn't whipped. One December day in 1965, the *Times Herald* police reporter called me.

"You ever know a guy named Jack Proctor?"

"Yeah."

"Shot himself this morning."

That afternoon, Shrake and Cartwright and some of us were at Nick's A.C. on the waterfront. By then, we knew the police blotter. He had gone to a hock shop on Deep Elm the night before, written a $21 check for a little .22 handgun (painstakingly filling in his checkbook stub correctly!), sat on his apartment couch the next morning, and when wife Betty went to the kitchen for more coffee, she said, he outs with the thing and pop. He was 58.

We drank a couple beers in silence, each reviewing his own mental file on Saintly Julien.

Finally, Shrake coughed.

"Son of a bitch could have called somebody."

There were nods around the table and, as I remember, that was all that was ever said.

INCREDIBLE PEOPLE

Requiem for an All-American

(*Dallas Morning News,* June 7, 1971)

Six months after they took the left leg of Freddie Steinmark, he returned to the Houston tumor clinic for another of his nerve-wracking checkups. The little Texas safety had to do this every three months, as do all victims of osteogenic sarcoma. He underwent blood tests and x-rays to determine if the dread malignancy might appear in other parts of his strong young body.

For several nights preceding his trips to M.D. Anderson Hospital, Freddie would stare at the ceiling. He knew the odds. He prayed for a miracle.

"They told me not to worry, but that's easy for them to say," Freddie said. "They're taking the x-rays, not getting them."

When Freddie would get a clean report, he would return joyously to the Texas campus and throw himself into another project with fierce energy. He took up golf, balancing himself on one leg while he swung. He learned to water ski. He went religiously to the Longhorn weight room to build up the rest of his body, as if muscle could hold off any return invasion of cancer cells. He worked his grades back to a B average. He made speeches and appearances. He wanted feverish activity to keep his mind occupied, so it wouldn't wander back to the calendar and the date of his next trip to Houston.

Last July a couple blurs showed up on x-rays of Freddie's lungs. It could be one of several things, the doctors told Freddie, we'll watch it close. A bit later, they told Freddie he would have to start a series of chemo-therapy treatments. He didn't change expression. But he guarded the news as if it were the atomic secret. He wanted no one to know. It was almost as if Freddie thought the treatments were a sign of personal weakness. The news might bring pity from his teammates and friends and, above all, he didn't want that.

• • •

The chemo-therapy consisted of six days of shots that, hopefully, would kill or arrest any fast-growing cancer cells. They make the patient frightfully nauseous. But he masked the trips and treatments from all, save a precious few. Scott Henderson, the linebacker and Freddie's apartment mate, knew but he respected the confidence.

One possible side effect of chemo-therapy shots is the loss of hair. Freddie had a long, thick black mane and he was proud of it. His teammates teasingly accused him of being a hippie. "Okay, you guys," he said. "I'm gonna help coach the freshmen defensive backs and just to show you how seriously I'm taking this job, I'll get rid of the hippy image. I'll get rid of all this hair. As a matter of fact, I'll just shave it all off, just to show you I'm not kidding."

So the Texas squad had a little ceremony in the locker room, and they all laughed and cheered as Bobby Wuensch shaved off the Steinmark hair. His teammates didn't realized he dreamed up this little act to hide the fact he was taking treatment that made his hair fall out. He kept his head shaved. Rick Troberman took note of the bald head and the missing leg and applied the nickname "Pirate." Freddie went along with the gag. He had his ear pierced and wore a gold ring in it for a while.

He shared his worry and concern with no one. But sometimes when you were in a conversation with Freddie, he would be staring at you vacantly with those enormous black eyes and there would be a silence, and he would say, "Excuse me, I guess I wasn't listening. What did you say?"

• • •

To the last, Freddie refused to accept the idea that the cancer had caught up with him and finally dragged him down. When he was hospitalized this last time in M.D. Anderson, he believed—at least outwardly—that he was there to have some fluid removed from his body. When his priest from Austin, Father Fred Bomar, walked quietly into Room 514W and sat down, Freddie looked at him narrowly.

"Have you got some business in Houston, Father?" he said. The priest said no, he just came down for a visit.

"Do you know something I don't know?" asked Freddie. The priest said no.

His friends thought it was rather a miracle, Freddie having played regularly on a national championship team with the tumor already gnawing at his leg, and had survived the amputation and returned to active life, had been able to move back into society, to tell people how he felt, to squeeze another 17 months out of precious life. Freddie didn't think it was a miracle; it was what an athlete was supposed to do, and now that same fierce competition kept him hanging on for days, weeks, after the average person would have let go. Doctors walked out of his room with tears in their eyes.

Two weeks ago, I visited the room. The shades were drawn. A television set suspended from the ceiling, with the volume off, flickered lifelessly with a soap opera. There was a skinny couch with bed pillows along one wall, where Freddie's mother, Gloria, and his girlfriend, Linda Wheeler, spent each day and his father spent each night. A vigil candle on a table burned 24 hours a day. Freddie was a gaunt shadow and his voice was about gone, and I had to bend close to hear him whisper, "I'm getting better."

Freddie has written a book about his experiences. It will be published this fall. The editor noticed after Freddie was hospitalized that he had not made a dedication of the book, and he asked to whom Freddie wanted to dedicate his story. Freddie said to the Lord, who had been so good to him.

The Essence of an Era

(Dallas Morning News, March 12, 1989)

Nearly as I can remember, Dorothy Lamour was not there. But she certainly would not have been out of place, with a red print sarong and a white hibiscus blossom in her flowing dark tresses.

She could have padded barefoot through the lush grass carpet under the rusty old palms, stepped around the fallen coconuts, so long on the ground that they had taken root in the tropical lushness and sent fresh young green shoots through the rotting husks. She could have emerged from the shadows onto the narrow beach, a clean, curving blend of white and beige, with hard coral crests on the jutting flanks.

The Caribbean waters, interrupted by an occasional long furl of whitecap, were blue as a baby's eyes. On the horizon, there was a dramatic break to a pale sky. The only signal of man was a sort of primitive umbrella, a thatched bowl atop an upright pole. Underneath, in a lawn chair embedded in sand, was a muscular man in flowery trunks, head bent in hypnotic fascination on an object in his lap. Occasionally, the man would lift his eyes and stare unseeingly at the horizon, then bend again in study.

Dorothy Lamour was missing all right, but had she paraded the beach in slinky seduction, she wouldn't have drawn a flick of notice. The man was Tom Landry of, oh, an eon past, and the object in his lap was a thick, looseleaf binder. It was a Dallas Cowboys' playbook.

This was an early edition of a perpetual volume about which Pete Gent, the renowned social commentator, once warned a rookie: "Don't read Landry's playbook. Everybody gets killed in the end."

Anyway, this is the most memorable Landry scene in my particular file, now that the nation seems to be canonizing the perpetual Cowboys' football coach on occasion of his abrupt firing by new Cowboy ownership.

Thinking back over the years, of course there is a montage of Landry snapshots, jumbled like a helter-skelter batch of clippings thrown in a cardboard packing crate, someday to be sorted out and mounted, tomorrow or the next day or the next year or the next decade or never. But this picture of Landry on the beach, a quarter-century ago, remains most prominently etched. I suppose it is most graphic because it was my first exposure to the man's dedication to his craft. It was the overture to an opera, a prologue to a novel. A peek inside.

To most of us stunned onlookers, it was almost unbelievable that a healthy male animal, in the midst of exotic Eden, would forsake the pleasures of the adventure to concentrate on drab X's and O's. Surely there was time for this in a drearier time and setting.

Maybe the young Cowboys coach was trying to impress someone? This thought crossed our minds. Club owner Clint Murchison was there; it was his private Bahamian island we were visiting. Perhaps Landry was showing off before Pete Rozelle, then the fledging NFL president who also was along. Or Bill MacPhail, then the boss of mighty CBS Sports. Or Amon Carter Jr., the late newspaper publisher, or Cowboys associates Tex Schramm, Larry Karl, Gil Brandt or the fun-loving rover boys, Bob Thompson and Bedford Wynne, or even the gaggle of newspaper wretches along for the ride.

After all, Landry had entered in earlier sybaritic activities on the stag outing. He stayed on the fringe of the general ragging and hoo-rahing and nighttime tippling, allowing a grin here and there.

In that same cove, one afternoon earlier, with the party people chest deep in soothing surf, natives wading out with balanced trays of a rum-coconut elixir, a Murchison sailor had buzzed a speedboat alongside the coral reef with brown slats jutting from the stern. Of these swashbuckling stalwarts, only one guy accepted the challenge. Suddenly we looked up, alerted by louder motor thrusts, and here was Landry arising

70

from the spray, to stay awkwardly but doggedly upright in his first try at water skis.

That very morning, we had sailed on two launches to nearby waters and yanked aboard all brands of prey, from shark to dolphin to grouper to kings. Someone counted a dozen variety of fish victim to our expert trolling. Even the rankest outdoorsman felt like Ernest Hemingway, high on the flying bridge, a live flipping rodtip under his hand and line singing like the Wichita lineman. We had come in for a lunch, conch salad and melon and cheese and iced tea on a cool veranda.

Then we were headed out again, all except Landry, who walked past the lodge with a half-embarrassed wave, playbook under his arm, walking down the rise to the palm grove and beach beyond. We stared in disbelief.

But as we amateur psychologists learned quickly, this was no act, no calculated call for attention, no attempt to impress. This was simply the Landry sanction. The theme. This was his modus operandi. He had relaxed for two days, and now it was time to punch the clock. To pay the piper.

Come to think of it, I am not sure Landry was even enjoying those first two days. That might have been the act. He may have preferred to be with his beloved playbook all the time.

But I do think he found it a bit easier to relax in those early days, before the Landry image began to build, like the gradual carving of faces on Mount Rushmore. I can remember when he would drop by the club's hospitality suite on road trips, he and Alicia, and actually have a Scotch—one Scotch—and listen politely to some of the banter. But we always had the feeling he had rather be somewhere else.

I also have seen Landry smile on a football field. You remember the story when Cornell Green intercepted a Don Meredith pass in practice, and Meredith, in mock rage, chased Green down the field beating him with his helmet while the squad laughed. Landry did not.

"Nothing funny ever happens on a football field," he said.

Many of us disagreed. We choose to think something funny

may happen at any time, on a football field or in a war or even at a funeral. Meredith, after his retirement, was asked if he would like his son to play for Landry.

"No," said Don. "I would rather he had some fun."

Dan Reeves, the Denver coach and former Cowboys player and assistant coach, on the subject: "Meredith had tremendous talent, but he played the game more for the fun of it than the seriousness of it. If he had been as dedicated as John Elway, no telling what he might have accomplished. Of course, that always led to friction with Coach Landry, who couldn't understand that type of thinking."

But that first Cowboys year, 1960, I saw Landry smile during business hours. At old Burnett Field, where the Cowboys trained, L.G. Dupre had trouble running a certain pass pattern, and he was furious at himself. He kept looking down at the grass, spitting and cursing himself. Apparently, it was a pattern employed mostly by Baltimore, where Dupre had spent many seasons.

"What's the matter, L.G.?" said Landry. "Is that a new pattern for you?" And the coach grinned as Dupre kept spitting and cursing. That was as close to banter as I ever heard the coach get.

Reeves tells of his rookie year, when the Cowboys were playing Cleveland in a big game. In a pileup, in front of the Cowboys' bench, Reeves suddenly screeched in pain and kicked viciously at Cleveland defender Paul Wiggin. Landry shouted at Reeves, "You'll get a penalty! You'll cost us the game!"

Reeves, livid, pointed at Wiggin. "He pinched me! He pinched me!" Landry grinned and turned away, presumably to keep from laughing. The officials laughed. In the huddle, somber Don Perkins said, "I'll get him back for you, Danny. I'll goose him when he ain't looking."

Of course, Landry never was a laughing boy, running around with a dribble glass and giving hotfoots. But he seemed to gravitate more into his waxen image as the Cowboys progressed, to a successful stage where they no longer were regarded as the helpless urchin abandoned on expansion's doorstep. With success, there also came occasional criticism, traditionally a curse of growth.

Perhaps that closer scrutiny by the industry's microscopes steeled the Landry armor plating. It was about that time, two decades ago, when the nickname "Mt. Landry" was coined in these scribblings. It seemed to fit the stolid, unflappable and dependable, durable object he had become. He was there, in his unflinching granite form, yesterday, today and tomorrow. And some sports diagnosticians, unable to penetrate that shell, resented it. Strange, the same veneer that made Ben Hogan intriguing and respected by millions, seemed to work the opposite with Landry. Some critics were angrily perplexed: We cut him, why doesn't he bleed?

In the face of mistakes, the coach seemed unperturbed. And like even the most confident, capable operators, he made mistakes. Or so it seemed to us Vaunted Experts. The indecision about quarterbacks, for example, the use of the Quarterback Shuttle, alternating Eddie LeBaron and Meredith, Roger Staubach and Craig Morton, this seemed an awkward arrangement, and it was only when Landry made a firm decision that his team seemed to roll. That's but one case. Another: Once during a halftime chastisement, Landry removed his Super Bowl ring and told the team he was embarrassed to wear it in view of its performance. Mistake. It made some veterans mad as blazes, figuring their accomplishment in the past stood alone and was earned and deserved and had no bearing to the day in question.

Landry is generally viewed as an honest, fortright gent, but in the fashion of all honest, fortright coaches, he was not above an occasional fib to protect his players. Once, he had removed Bob Hayes from the starting lineup for some malfunction. His explanation afterward was that Hayes was injured, unable to play. Yet some of us remembered and later confirmed by films that Hayes indeed had played on kicking teams, one of the more hazardous assignments and certainly one spared any injured man. A check of the NFL office failed

73

to show any injury report on Hayes, which league rules required. But league spokesmen, made aware of the contrast in stories, later called and said, well, maybe they had overlooked the report. A cover-up, obviously. Landry was protecting Hayes by camouflaging his disciplinary action.

Then, there was the difficult Duane Thomas season, when the moody tailback refused to speak to anyone—media, coaches, teammates, trainers, doctors, whomever. The Cowboys went to, and won, the Super Bowl that year while Landry steadfastly denied Thomas' monk act, even his missing a Super Bowl practice, by any way distracted other players. He did this before the national media gathered at the Super Bowl. Yet after the game, he reversed his story, stating that indeed Thomas was a distraction and that he and the team never again would go through that experience. Thomas, in a rambling broadcast diatribe, had described his coach as "a plastic man," and, frankly, there were those who thought it a fairly credible description.

And yet, through the Thomas trials, Landry showed another of his engraved characteristics—patience.

By that time, Reeves was an assistant coach. He remembered, "Patience was one of the reasons Dallas won its first Super Bowl. Coach Landry had patience with Duane Thomas when a lot of us just wanted to get rid of him. He also had patience with us."

Landry seldom admitted mistakes; instead, he had a reason for this and that. Rationalization, we called it. The Great Rationalizer. But there was a moment where Landry let down his Iron Curtain just a bit, when he confessed to bewilderment and confusion. This instance was the second of my most memorable moments in the Landry association.

This came in 1968, after his Cowboys had attained major status. In truth, they were "America's Team," a label that secretly pleased Landry as much as it delighted Tex Schramm. The year before, the nation's heart bled when the poor, thin-blooded fledglings from the Sunshine Belt had barely lost to big, brawny, invincible Green Bay in the infamous Ice Bowl.

And now the following December, Landry took his team to Cleveland for the Eastern championship game. The Cowboys had beaten the Browns with little trouble earlier in the season.

Yet for some weird reason, Landry's team could not function that day. In fact, the Cowboys were so amateurishly inept that the Browns stood on the sideline and hooted their ridicule.

On the chartered plane homeward, Landry's face was haggard and drawn. When media gathered around his seat, he could not explain, and for once, he did not attempt to rationalize. He was mystified and admitted it and said he did not know the answer. He looked forelorn and helpless, like a man committed to the gallows on the morrow. He sat immobile in his seat and looked downward for most of the trip, filled with who knows how much self-doubt and uncertainty.

This was on December 21. And as the plane trundled to its gate, Landry unbuckled his seat belt, stood facing the rear of the plane, and as his squad filed slowly past en route to the front exit, he shook hands with each, thanked him for the season and wished him and family a Merry Christmas. Each, individually. It was almost a ceremony. I don't know about the rest of the witnesses, but at no time in 30 years had I seen Landry show so much inner strength.

The third impression I will take away from the Landry years was his constant courtesy and utter lack of individual resentment toward his media critics. After a defeat on the road, there was none of these curt answers and angry stompoffs as Mike Ditka has been known to do, and Bill Parcells and Chuck Noll and John McKay and even Vince Lombardi was capable of doing. Landry always met with familiar and strange reporters alike and gave thoughtful attention to questions, no matter the downgrading implications. Regular Cowboys media took this for granted; foreign press continually was impressed and appreciative. And on the local front, Landry made no distinction between critics who might call him senile and faltering and downright dumb, and those less impetuous.

The late sportswriter Dick Young once wrote a splendid (I

INCREDIBLE PEOPLE

thought) parable illustrating Leo Durocher's calloused insensitivity. Imagine Durocher walking across the Brooklyn Bridge at night, stopped by a panhandler who demands money. Durocher refuses, whereupon the guy heaves the manager over the rail. Durocher hits the water below and starts yelling for help. A fellow on the bank hears the cries, jumps in, swims to Durocher, tows him back to land and saves his life.

The next day, wrote Young, Durocher would not know the one man from the other.

Not true with Landry. He would know, he just wouldn't show it.

The fourth indelible impression was one that seems to support a secret theory that Landry, impassive and reserved as he is, loves the limelight. Loves it. And will eventually bring him to surface again in public life in some fashion.

A game in St. Louis. The team hotel was just across the street from Busch Stadium, maybe 150 steps. I happened on the scene early, standing on a higher ramp, when I noticed a strange wad of humanity moving gradually across the street. Slowly, like lava flowing. I looked closer, and there at the core of the mass was a familiar snapbrim hat and blue suede-cloth jacket. Landry was moving along a halfstep at a time, signing autographs. There were cops there to hustle players and coaches across the street, to form protective corridors from the curious onlookers. But Landry shrugged off the escort. He was by himself, and wherein most so-called celebrities consider autographing a crashing bore, I had the strong suspicion that he loved it.

But the last and probably strongest impression I will take away from the Landry era—and it deserves to be labeled an era—was his steadfast and eternal religious faith. He never pushed his religion, he was no loud "Christer," as jocks call it, other than to advise his players on priority: God, family, team, in that unmistakable, unalterable order.

Some may brand it a Polyanna theory, but it is the belief here that Landry's unyielding faith and devout trust in God contributed to his strength. Not just contributed, it is his strength. He feeds off it. It has sustained Landry through bad times as well as good, and it is the primary reason he seemed impervious to criticism and doubt and, in later years, downright slander.

Perhaps that faith fueled his almighty rationalization. Perhaps what some of us occasionally mistook for a blind ego and sometimes irritating confidence actually was the inner rod of religious faith. If so, it will see him through this recent haymaker to his pride.

Maybe coaching did pass him by, for he was slow to change, and perhaps the ridiculous complications of modern play was too much for any man to handle alone, as he stubbornly tried to do. But he eventually will enter the sports history books as a successful and innovative coach.

The notations won't mention that Tom Landry was a strong, decent and good human, which, to some of us, is infinitely more important. Will Rogers once said that the trouble with many heroes is that they overstay. And the wise guys will shrug in the calloused pressbox and in the impatient stadiums, just as they say in corporate board rooms: What the heck, he was here and now he's gone, so set 'em up in the other alley. But some of us, realists as well as romanticists, will remember and salute.

Art of Communication

The Gift of Gab or Lack Thereof

One Art Eluded Jefferson

(*Dallas Morning News,* February 27, 1997)

Along with a goodly portion of the populace, I went back to school during Ken Burns' PBS special on Thomas Jefferson. We all were exposed to Mr. Jefferson during history classes, when we weren't flipping spitballs, but there were aspects of this remarkable man that had slipped through the memory cracks.

You were stunned at the fellow's scope when you learned that he taught himself Greek and Latin and how to play the violin at an age when most of us were studying hide-and-seek. He became a scientist, astrologer, astronomer, architect, farmer, carpenter, ironworker, builder, writer, horticulturist, viticulturist, butcher, baker, candlestick maker, statesman, inventor and not a bad hand around the ladies.

Mr. Thomas Jefferson could do dang near anything but make a speech, thereby endearing himself to a vast army of us stuttering slobs.

He had a lisp and a high-pitched, nasal voice that fell unpleasantly upon surrounding ears, including his own. So, with admirable restraint, he mostly kept his trap shut. Historians say that even when he was president, he seldom spoke more than two sentences at a time. Lo, may his presidential tribe increase.

• • •

If this sounds expertish on speeches, it is for solid reason. At last audit, I have personally heard 18 zillion, 2,141 billion, 540 million, 2,001 speeches in my lifetime. I deem this enough to qualify as a shadetree judge of same. Certainly, it is enough to learn that the art of speechmaking—*good* speechmaking—is a rare and enviable skill. As in Mr. Jefferson's case, the skill is not a derivative of any other talent. It is not a byproduct but rather a separate art unto itself.

Speeches are influential, all too often, because of the style

81

and decibels with which they are delivered, rather than content. You have only to hark back to the last presidential election. Bill Clinton is as glib as any siding salesman, while poor Bob Dole couldn't speak his way out of a paper sack. Certainly, this swayed voters, perhaps as much as the issues involved, whatever they were.

Mr. Clinton once expounded: "You can put wings on a pig, but you can't make him an eagle."

This *sounded* profound, leading Mark Russell to remark, "I have no idea what that means, but it's about as close to the Gettysburg Address as we're gonna get."

• • •

Jesse Jackson is a spellbinder whiz, and Pat Buchanan is both glib and meaty. Ann Richards has the gift. Edward Bennett Williams, the late Washington lawyer, was a masterful speaker, both in content and delivery, and most remarkable, he never used a note. Last spring, I heard Grant Teaff speak to a college graduating class—maybe 25 minutes of smooth flow, and he, too, never used a note. Said he never had.

I heard two other football coaches, Vince Lombardi and Woody Hayes, who were polished, powerful speakers, both in syntax and delivery. They seldom mentioned football.

Other sports luminaries, along with TV personalities, are professional speakers, booked on regular circuits. One such chain features Bobby Knight, the basketball icon, and horse trainer D. Wayne Lucas, who handles the language and establishes points equally well. A regular on the loop is Lou Holtz, late of Notre Dame, and, if you nod off, he'll do a couple of magic tricks for you. The late Duffy Daugherty spoke far and wide but mostly shallow. He always included an inspirational poem: "If you can't be a moon, be a star." Most of these popular motivational speeches seem to be a string of parables, with little substance.

The best speaker I ever heard, ever, in delivery, clarity, drama, content and message was Oliver North. I caught him on one of those C-Span deals when he was addressing correspondents of some nature, and I was fascinated. I know naught of Mr. North's honesty or character or whatever, but he is one dynamite speaker.

This, of course, deviates from the yardstick applied to podiums the land over. The ideal speaker, they say, is one whose plane leaves in 30 minutes.

Rabbit Ears Blight: From Splitting Hairs to Splitting Hares

(*Dallas Morning News,* May 1, 1997)

The line, as I recall, first appeared on the silver screen in a prison movie called *Cool Hand Luke,* with Paul Newman or one of those chaps.

"What we have here," said a guard, "is a failure to communicate." Or maybe Paul Newman said it or whoever. What the line expresses may describe today's written or spoken communication. The golfer Fuzzy Zoeller, formerly a carefree soul, discovered this the other day when he mentioned fried chicken and collard greens in the same paragraph with young mixed-blood golfer Tiger Woods. Well, sir, the sky fell.

Had Mr. Zoeller made the remark in the locker room, there probably would have been giggles all around, including from Tiger Woods. That Fuzzy, he's a card.

But then, when the wisecrack circulated, the zealous monitors of Political Correctness turned a double flip. The squawk shows frothed with delight, and Mr. Zoeller found himself in quicksand. Uncharacteristically somber, he made a public apology. His supermart sponsor, obviously frightened of customer repercussions, sprinted to the podium with a public dismissal of Mr. Zoeller. Hung the fellow out to dry.

At any rate, that uproar demonstrates the tenuous line that communicators must walk these days. Even a dumb, thoughtless gag shakes the walls around us.

• • •

Little ole me, I have had similar experiences, one involving, coincidentally, a reference to food. When a Cowboy lineman had an obvious weight surplus, I mentioned pork chops being a factor, and newspaper copy editors promptly went into a tizzy. Never mind that the remark was not mine but a direct quote from a Cowboy scout who also happened to be black. It might "offend somebody," said the nervous nellies.

The words were written in all innocence; I had never thought of pork chops having a racial connotation. Heck, I had eaten pork chops for breakfast that very day, a favorite meal of mine. Besides, this was a direct quote from someone else, contained in the proper punctuation and all that. I thought the whole concern just a bit ridiculous, but in retrospect, the monitors were probably right. These are those sort of times. No sense pushing the envelope, especially in a nondescript sports essay.

Another time, I used the term Nips in a column, again in all innocence. Another monitor called to say the word was offensive to Japanese. Golly, I was under the impression that Nippon was another name for Japan and that the term was as harmless as using "Yanks" for us gallant lads. Perhaps I should have known better, but having been around during the Late Hate, perhaps I was too calloused.

More recently, I wrote "squaw" in some harmless parable. I know of no hack around here any more sympathetic to the Native American cause than old buster here. But the post brought several warm letters, protesting that the word was derogatory to women of the tribes. I bet you didn't know that.

• • •

Of course, all memories include the results of remarks made by Jimmy the Greek Snyder and Al Campanis, both of whom I knew for years. Believe me, each was so very proud of his public status that he would never, never knowingly make *any* observation, racial or otherwise, to threaten it. But both lost their jobs as a result.

Last week, TV boxing analyst Larry Merchant made some chance remark about mariachi music played at the Oscar De La Hoya-Pernell Whittaker fight and returned to the cameras a few days later to apologize for any racial insult that some chose to interpret therein.

There once was a sports slang term, "rabbit ears," for

ART OF COMMUNICATION

those who were eager to react to real or imagined slights. So it may be assumed that the Rabbit Ears Blight is upon us. Possibly you can understand the apprehension within ranks of reporters and editors and commentators, beset with apprehension that every word or phrase or sentence must pass under a grave microscope before being sailed toward the public, vulnerable as a skeet target. So all we can say to the latest victim: Welcome to the docks, Fuzzy, the Purple Hearts are over there on the bar.

Discourse Sinks Under Weight of Gravitas

(Dallas Morning News, August 17, 2000)

Bro. Dave Gardner, our favorite philosopher, was reviewing his fractured parable of David and Goliath.

Little David, said Bro. Dave, was taking some light bread and gravy sandwiches to his big brothers, who were dug in, fighting the Philadelphians.

"How's it going, big brothers, you whupping up on the Philadelphians?"

"Naw," said the disheartened brothers. "They done run a giant in on us."

Well, some of us know the feeling. After we monitored the spoutings from convention rostrums and after we memorized the customary idioms and tired old catch phrases, the pundits done run a new word in on us.

In the late stages of the Republican confab, *gravitas* began cropping up in convention coverage. GRAUVE-eee-tas. Rhymes with bobby socks or dang near.

George W. Bush may have been a good governor, but he doesn't have the *gravitas* a president needs. Dick Cheney was added to the ticket because he lends *gravitas* to the Republican cause.

• • •

Following the Philadelphia convention, Prof. Rush Limbaugh, the self-styled radio expert on all things political, ridiculed fellow pundits who hastened to use *gravitas* in their commentaries.

He played a tape with clips from a dozen highdomes using the word over and over. Bush gravitas this, Bush gravitas that. Here a gravitas, there a gravitas, everywhere a gravitas.

Clearly, it was the media's favorite catchword for the

nonce, and the pols picked it up. The former New York governor got his jollies from the word.

"I think the governor was looking for someone with gravitas," said Mario Cuomo, "because he has been accused of not having sufficient gravitas for the presidency."

Mr. Cumo added a warning: "Unfortunately, you can't graft gravitas."

The *Washington Times* editorialized, "The positions Mr. Bush has enunciated on defense and foreign policy ... reveal the Texas governor to have gravitas of his own."

Newsday had a headline: "Bush shoots for a sense of gravitas on ticket."

It sorta reminded you of when the word *detente* entered the international political language. Sent us common folk to Mr. Merriam and Mr. Webster, didn't it?

Obviously, the learned commentators consider gravitas a common word, something abounding in everyday conversation.

Hey, Eddie, how's your gravitas these days? Getting better, thank you. I rubbed a little kerosene on it, and that sucker dried up.

Mildred, doesn't this pie have a different flavor? Yes, I found some fresh gravitas in the produce department.

• • •

The stout chaps of our weekly literary clutch, language students all, were familiar with the word. Sure they were. One said he had a cousin busted for trying to bring gravitas in from Juarez.

Oh, no, said a Latin student, the word comes from gravity. Like that guy Newton wrote, Mr. Cheney will keep Mr. Bush from taking naps under apple trees.

Then, like a pesky vine, the word crept into the Democrat vocabulary. After Sen. Joe Lieberman caught the vice presidential bouquet, one goldythroat declared, "If Al Gore wanted gravitas, he would have picked George Mitchell."

Yet another expert referred to Mr. Gore's obvious link to

the Oval Office Romeo when he offered, "Lieberman brings 'ethical' gravitas to the ticket." (Ethical gravitas, as opposed to *un*-ethical gravitas?)

Anyway, your crack reporter here, after diligent research in several dictionaries, some too heavy to lift, found gravitas to be a Latin term tied in with gravity and means "high seriousness in a person's bearing or in the treatment of a subject." Further, the term first made its appearance in this country in 1924, which, obviously, is the year we all missed class.

Politics and Government

Of Mice and Presidents and Others in Charge

We've Almost Quit Listening to Candidates

(*Dallas Morning News,* February 29, 1996)

Will Rogers, the cracker-barrel sage of his time, began most commentaries with "All I know is what I read in the papers." Of course, if Mr. Rogers were alive today, he would be saying, "All I know is what I see on television."

Especially is this true when we go about electing the big cheese of the land. We have become so sensitive, so perceptive, so darned *electronic* that we can look at a fellow on the tube and tell if he would make a decent president or if he is apt to lock the door to the Oval Office and set fire to the cat. Don't forget, pundits judged that Richard Nixon lost the 1960 presidential race to John Kennedy because his 5 o'clock shadow was accentuated by television lights to give him a sinister look. He lost by a whisker?

The Republican forays through Iowa and New Hampshire afforded a good opportunity to study expressions and inflections and gestures, for there was very little verbal content. Actually, the "debates" were embarrassing to us clods on the couch, as if we were guests at a party and inadvertently walked into a room where the host and hostesses were having a spirited argument. Supposedly, these were men dedicated to the same Republican principles, and they were acting like a dog sled team—bound by the same harness but at vicious odds when a single bone was tossed among them.

So in resignation, we watched for these little facial hints, these gestures, the furrows in the noble forehead as the candidate considers some question, the tone of voice. The sincerity of the perpetual smile on the missus' face in the background.

Obviously, Pat Buchanan was the *visual* winner. He *looks* like a man who would be named Pat Buchanan. He is glib, he has the writer's gift for catchy phrases, he speaks distinctly and firmly, even belligerently, and he punches his right hand for emphasis and isn't awkward at it. He has been accused of looking mean, so he apparently makes an effort to laugh occasionally, but the sound is forced and grating.

Obviously, the other candidates regard Mr. Buchanan as a rogue tiger at the watering hole, an angry man with a chip on his shoulder. If so, his rising support indicates there are a number of angry folks out there. You must say this for Mr. Buchanan: He ain't afraid.

Steve Forbes was soft and doughy, and his voice was nice and forgettable. He seemed serenely unworried, as, indeed, any chap with a full plate is wont to do.

Lamar Alexander appeared pleasant and excited to be in this championship bracket. Almost all males can relate with Mr. Alexander; any adult man who ever opened a Christmas gift has one of those plaid flannel shirts in his closet. It may indicate Mr. Alexander's practicality that he has found a use for the danged thing.

● ● ●

Poor Bob Dole. It would seem his Washington experience makes him best equipped to run things, with all his pals in the Republican Congress. The old guard probably will rally around and award him the nomination. But the old campaigner is rather short in the rhetoric department. His words emerge dry and lifeless, and he has the misfortune of appearing dour and humorless.

Mr. Dole may remind you of a gifted writer who is a woeful orator. Plus, he is 72, and you sense that when he finally shuts his hotel bedroom door at night, shucks his shoes, loosens his belt, rubs some feeling into his wounded right hand and collapses his aching back in the overstuffed chair, the question must cross his mind: Who needs this mess?

Mostly, Mr. Dole appears a big lame elk trying to get back to his herd while a wolf pack snaps at his flanks. He is miffed at the lack of respect from the other chaps, and he cannot help—despite himself—yapping back at his tormentors. Why, certainly he is best equipped for the job, he seems to be saying, so why must we endure this charade? *This is demeaning to me. I have long been a good soldier in the field, and now that they're about to pin the stars on my shoulder, here are some shavetails yelling in the balcony. How dare they?*

The thing is far from over, and there is yet a strong definition of the Republican path. Except for one facet. With his group of supporters, Pat Buchanan attempted to sing *God Bless America* and, in doing so, surely blew the musicians' vote. Ole Pat might carry a pitchfork, but he cannot carry a tune.

Significance Can Be Hard to Find

(Dallas Morning News, August 15, 1996)

In all justice, the blame could be assigned to Walter Red Smith, the late sports essayist.

In 1956, some editor at the *New York Tribune* was smitten with a novel idea. The political conventions were coming up, and this editor suggested that Mr. Smith be added to the paper's coverage of same.

Mr. Smith had the enviable talent to write wryly about any subject, and the editors reasoned, rightly, that political conventions need to be viewed with as much wryness as could be mustered. At the convention, as could be expected, Mr. Smith composed exceptional wryness.

Well, four years later, when the conventions came around, several newspapers played copycat with sports columnists. Which is why ole buster here was paroled from jock topics long enough to attend the 1960 Democratic confab in Los Angeles.

The assignment was more of a revelation than an education, not unlike the first viewing of a tag team rassle match. To put it kindly, there was ample posturing, thank you very much.

• • •

Now, this was before political media fangs were as obvious as in today's press rows. Also, the experts came in flocks rather than floods. But I was fascinated with these editorial pundits and the great seriousness with which they took themselves.

I was reminded of the time his editors sent Will Rogers to observe a political convention. Some of the stiff-necked journalists were scornful of Mr. Rogers' assignment.

One haughty wiseman, employed by the same newspaper syndicate as Mr. Rogers, grudgingly acknowledged his presence. "I assume you are here to write your funny little pieces," said Mr. Highdome. "Well, if I find anything humorous, I will let you know."

"That's very kind of you," said Our Will. "If I find anything serious, I'll let *you* know."

• • •

I can remember the press mob in the Biltmore Hotel corridor outside Lyndon Johnson's suites. TV cables, a rather new arrival, slithered on the floor like bewildered tree snakes. Anxious reporters, pads and pens at the ready, paced like expectant fathers.

One chap on the early watch reported that at approximately 7:58 A.M., Sen. Johnson had stuck his head out of a door and that he was wearing a bathrobe and his hair was tousled.

Reporters absorbed this news soberly enough. Nowadays, of course, Geraldo and Sally Jesse would speculate at length on whether it was the senator's *own* door.

Later, Sen. Johnson popped out of a room in a black silk suit and a tailored, high-collared blue shirt, jowls freshly shaven and powdered and hair slick as a country club bartender.

"What's the news, senator?" asked one expert, a chap with obvious aforethought.

"More of the same," said the candidate. "No change." He smiled pleasantly as he popped through another door.

"Whadee say? Whadee say?" yelled latecomers.

A delegate emerged from the Johnson headquarter suite. He was quite willing to be interviewed. He said his name was Andrew Campbell from Indiana.

"Spell it like you do the soup," he said helpfully.

Well, Mr. Campbell, are there any new developments?

"I'd say that things are picking up on the first ballot," said the delegate from Indiana.

In what direction, Mr. Campbell?

"That depends on how things go on the first ballot," he said. Pens flew across pads.

This appeared to be significant, and I should have been taking notes. But political novice as I was, I found myself instead thinking back to the convention's noisy opening session.

Ole Sam Rayburn, the Texas bald eagle and Sen. Johnson's guru, sat stolidly in a wooden folding chair at the end of a row in the Texas representation. Delegates milled about him constantly; occasionally, one would bend to talk in his ear. Ole Sam never spoke nor changed his dour expression.

From time to time, he would reach under his chair for a white Styrofoam cup, sip slowly and just as deliberately, return it to the floor under his rump. To show you how the inexpert mind works, I found myself wondering what was in that cup.

Craving a Place in History

(Dallas Morning News, March 20, 1997)

On two particular points, historians all agree. One: Tyrus Cobb was among the top half-dozen baseball players ever. On the other hand, he also was the most miserable human being. Especially in his later years did Mr. Cobb delight in exposing himself as a drunken bully, profane and cruel, crude, rude and booed. And yet with all that antagonism boiling inside, Mr. Cobb had one dominant human trait, perhaps the only one in his locker. According to biographer Al Stump, the old brute worried about his memorial niche.

"Do you think they'll remember me?" he asked, rather piteously, in his death wait.

Another example comes to mind. Elston Brooks, whom we fondly called Lunchmeat, was a Fort Worth newspaperman with a rare sense of humor. He was dying and took a grievous time doing it. However, in his last days in the hospital, he wrote postcards to a few pals, with instructions to someone, a nurse perhaps or his wife, to mail them after his funeral.

The handwritten message was something like: "It's nice up here. Elvis says hi."

Lunchmeat wanted very much to be remembered with humor rather than sadness, and, indeed, he was and is.

• • •

Considering those examples, one wonders what goes through Bill Clinton's mind these days. You sense that the man wants so desperately to be remembered kindly.

Certainly every president does; every president covets a respected place in world history. It is an integral part of the ego that makes one seek the office in the first place. Maybe it's not a strong factor in the beginning; perhaps it is a thirst for power that first drives a man toward the office. But a hunger for a lingering good image becomes a vital part of that ego, an obsession, especially in his last months in the Oval Office.

Even Lyndon Johnson, who could be mean and vindictive with the worst, was jealous of his place in history. He wanted to be remembered as a great humanitarian rather than a ruthless schemer in Vietnam doings. He was frustrated that he couldn't arrange it. Harry Truman, who often seemed surprised that the country could be run on common sense, gloried in his post-presidential esteem. Richard Nixon thirsted for respect and, behind closed doors, bristled meanly at lack of same. If you believe his biographers, he went to his crypt feeling grossly unappreciated.

Jimmy Carter, perhaps after he left the White House, wanted to embellish his bland image. This probably is what leads him to intervene, usually uninvited, in international peacemaking attempts.

• • •

This must be a gnawing inside Bill Clinton. More than any other postwar president, he seems to crave popularity. Perhaps that is the reason he changes approaches so often, trying to tack with whatever popular wind is blowing at the moment.

His own brother, I thought, once had a good illustration: that if Brother Bill were in a room, speaking to 30 people, and if he convinced 29 of them, he still would be bothered it wasn't unanimous.

In the best of all Clinton worlds, he would have this last term to endear himself to the populace, to win over that 30th person, to polish his place in history. Fat chance. Despite citizen approval in those vague polls, the folks who disapprove of him *really* disapprove. Those who hate Slick Willie *really* hate him. And they seem to find new reasons every day.

When Ronald Reagan goofed, his detractors cracked jokes, but they found it hard to harbor intense hatred for the man. With the anti-Clintons, there's not a chuckle in a carload.

This must be a growing frustration to the Clinton clan, which realizes that the coveted popularity will be denied him in the history books and memories of The Great Unwashed and that the very best epitaph he can hope for is a sneer.

On the other hand, perhaps the president fits in the traditional oilfield story, about the old wildcatter who found himself being buried by expenses and likened himself to a foraging rodent.

"I'm no longer interested in the cheese," he said. "I'm just trying to get out of the trap."

Our Children's Future Holds Us Hostage

(Dallas Morning News, October 15, 1998)

Suffer the little children, says the Good Book, for theirs is the kingdom of heaven. Something like that.

With all respect and proper reverence, may I suggest an impudent addendum to the word from St. Matthew? Blessed are the little children for they shall be a dominant part of every political speech from every stump from here to Juneau.

Surely you notice. "Our children and grandchildren" has replaced Motherhood and Apple Pie as the stentorian specialty of the American politico. We don't hear Liberty and Freedom nearly as much these days as we hear the clarion call for "our children and grandchildren."

"Our children are our greatest natural resource" is also the greatest natural bray. The declaration usually is accompanied by the great thump of a clenched fist upon the rostrum and a righteous glare from the orator. The phrase rolls off the political tongue with the thunder of Winston Churchill's gallant declarations during Dunkirk.

The statement defies contradiction. What are you going to say? "To hell with 40 years from now, let's get the car paid off." You may think it, but you don't say it out loud.

The children seem the only concern shared by the various parties, whether Republican, Democrat, Reform, Libertarian, Independent, Bull Moose, VFW or the Committee to Legalize Slots in Pensacola. Well, maybe not the *only* mutual concern, but it's the one that monopolizes the podiums. The statesmen also may oppose earthquakes, diphtheria and flat tires on the freeway, but these are lucky to get a mention, even if the speech goes into overtime.

• • •

Listen to political commercials at any level. They all feature your children. George W. Bush, in his race for Texas governor, is determined to have them reading *Pilgrim's Progress* by the third grade and says so right there on the tube. Garry Mauro wants to decrease sizes of classes and give all teachers a handsome raise. Somehow, one doubts that anyone running for any governorship in the land fails to endorse a raise for schoolteachers. (The fact that the teachers and their unions are a formidable voting bloc is probably just incidental.)

Running for lieutenant governor, Rick Perry says, "Educating our children is the single most important thing we intend to do." His opponent, John Sharp, accuses him of "putting his politics ahead of our kids."

Dallas Rep. Martin Frost declares war on "predators who prey on our children." He didn't mention their parents.

Ross Perot, in his spasmodic rantings against Washington, keeps referring to the great financial burden that will bankrupt "our children." There are those who question the use of the plural pronoun. They doubt, frankly, that the Perot progeny will ever lack for bread and beans.

• • •

What we have here, of course, is a bulletproof principle. If you damn pollution, you might offend smokestack factories. If you endorsed a flat tax or a sales tax, you could enrage those who make livings in income taxation. If you take a firm stand on immigration, regardless of which side, some outcries will be heard from the audience.

But children—ah, no one dares oppose any move that may possibly, even remotely, benefit our children. It is the absolute foolproof political path.

It may take a geezer to remember, but there was a time when the modus operandi was to raise large families, lots of sons and daughters, so when the time came, there would be enough man-power to take care of mama and papa in their old age.

Somewhere along the line, the equation seems to have switched sides. This, despite the possible secret suspicion that your chillun will handle things just fine on their own, just as their fathers did in their day and their grandfathers before that.

103

Zippergate Left Many Winners

(*Dallas Morning News,* February 18, 1999)

It should come as some relief to discover, from this unreliable source, that all is not lost. *Some* body wins.

For months, The Addled Majority has been lectured that there are only losers in the Beltway Bedroom Follies. There's an old song: "Nobody Wins in the Game of Broken Hearts." It seemed to fit.

Republicans are seen as posturing opportunists, collapsing into vindictive rhetoric at the thrust of a microphone. Historians may record Democrats as stubborn defenders of a skunk works.

The principals will be besmirched, the supporting cast will be tainted, Ken Starr and his prosecutors will live in infamy. And us common slobs, uneasy with the tawdry scenario, will feel it most of all.

It is ever thus. The hoi polloi do most of the suffering, no matter the nature of conflict. Common folk are not as resilient as politicos, whose survival, like that of a turtle, depends on armored plating. But in the Oval Office Lie Fest, the ill effects vault the moat into the castle. The gentry likewise feel the pain. Everybody loses?

• • •

Well, it says here, however inexpertly, that there will be some winners after all. There usually are, regardless of the catastrophe. A volcano buries a village, but builders rush in, riding their trusty bulldozers and cement mixers. A deadly heat wave strikes, and air-conditioner sales double.

The Gulf War cost everybody, especially bewildered tax-payers. But how about the specialists brought in to bring Kuwait's burning oil wells under control? Did they work for free?

The major loser in this current mess, you would think, is

Bill Clinton himself. Not materially. His legal expenses have gone through the roof, but there's always some wealthy patron to pick up the tab. Mr. Clinton seems to have an uncommon number of these.

Regardless of wrist slaps, the president's major loss is his legacy. Traditionally, legacy becomes important to White Housers, especially as they pack to leave. Jimmy Carter and George Bush found it so. Certainly no president wants to enter history books as a randy reprobate who dragged the office through its slimiest days.

But remember that Mr. Clinton will be one of the youngest ex-presidents ever. The guess here is that he will shrug off the stigma, write a book or two, lecture for $100,000 per pop and keep on smiling, patting backs and pinching posteriors. He will accentuate the positive, eliminate the negative and won't mess with Mr. Inbetween. The fellow is a survivor, and in some perverse way, the black eye may add to his mystique.

• • •

Ken Starr? He also will make the lecture circuit and write a book. Heck, *every*body will write a book. Monica Lewinsky will make $10 million with her account, even though it may be as innocent as Little Miss Muffett. Don't worry about this young woman.

Linda Tripp? She won't do as well as Little Miss Victim, but she will have salable memoirs, spiced up with other tidbits gathered through her years.

The squawk show yappers? They have already profited greatly by this mess. Ready-made topics. Guests frothing to appear. Same with pollsters. Never have pollsters been so busy, so in demand, so well-paid, despite the fact that they are mythical to most of us.

It could be that all female politicians will benefit from the negative exposure of their male counterparts involved in this mess. But most of all, the single gainer in all this plot, silly as it sounds, may be Hillary Clinton. If true, as commonly reported, that Mrs. Clinton has long tolerated her spouse's rovings so long as they remained hidden and that she always thirsted for power, for prominence and for a role as a major player, then she could be the biggest winner of all. Look for her somewhere in the government. Chances are excellent she will not fade gently into the night.

In the final reckoning, there could be many winners. It may be left for us common folk to alter a line from the late Walt Kelly, the Pogo philosopher: We have met the losers, and they is us.

BLACKIE SHERROD AT LARGE

"Doctors" Have Been Spinning Since 1839

(*Dallas Morning News,* February 25, 1999)

Being of a skeptical profession, we have long suspected that someone was messing with our minds. Oh, they are not brain-washing us to a maniacal degree, like in *The Manchurian Candidate.* But they throw us a bucket of broccoli, tell us it is strawberry shortcake and expect us to take a bite. Most of us do.

These strategists are known as *spin doctors,* a term that has crept stealthily into our language. According to the *New Dictionary of American Slang,* a *spin doctor* is "an adviser who imparts a partisan analysis or slants a story for the media." The term stems from the "spin" a pool player or a baseball pitcher uses, giving the ball a deviant route.

Spin doctors treat the public like a hypnotist's foil. They present images with such deftness that John Doe thinks it is his own expert deduction.

Example: The president and missus alight from their heli-copter on the south lawn, greeted by a bounding Irish setter. (The animal probably has been taught that his master has a goodie hidden in his hand.) What a warm scene: president and faithful dog traipsing across the greensward.

But skeptics sneer: Yeah, in the face of the Oval Office Follies, the spin doctors sought to soften the president's image, so they got him a dog in midterm. A homebody with loving dog. What could be more true blue?

Besides, it gives the fellow something to do with his hands, since Hillary Clinton seems to have stopped holding hands with her husband in such exercises.

• • •

For his 1995 vacation, reports the *New Yorker,* the presi-dent planned to play golf on Martha's Vineyard. But spin doc-tor Dick Morris saw golf as "a Republican sport" and instead sent the president hiking in the Rockies, sleeping in a tent and being bitten by insects of the region. By dawgies, that feller is one of us!

Some devout skeptics even believe that, on four occasions, the spin doctors ordered bombs dropped on Mideast aspirin factories and such to keep the Six O'Clock News from concentrating on Mr. Clinton's intramural sport.

. . .

There is a tendency to place spin doctors as a product of television, that they are a comparatively new breed. Then along comes historian Richard Shenkman, in his book *Presidential Ambition,* to nail the origin.

In 1839, the Whigs chose William Henry Harrison to run against White House incumbent Martin Van Buren. Mr. Harrison was old and tired, and he had no views, which campaign managers considered a plus. They told him to say nothing. What he had was a nickname: Tippecanoe, gained 30 years before by defeating the Shawnee near Tippecanoe Creek, Ind.

"The campaign wouldn't be about issues at all," writes Mr. Shenkman, "it would be about a personality, a celebrity."

The Whig strategists coined a slogan: "Tippecanoe and Tyler, too!" (John Tyler was the vice presidential candidate.) They had songs and jingles written.

When a Democrat slurred Mr. Harrison by saying he was better fit for a log cabin and a jar of bourbon, the managers whooped with delight. They quickly adopted the log cabin as the symbol of the party, and log cabin mania spread. Ole Tippecanoe, log cabin to White House! A natural.

(Actually, Mr. Harrison had been born in a lovely two-story mansion on the James River and wouldn't know a log cabin from a two-car garage.)

"Truth didn't count for anything in a campaign anymore," writes Mr. Shenkman. "It was all theater. Image. Slogans. Whatever the public would buy. Trickery became common. The lesson was, to win, a party had to manipulate popular opinion any way it could. In the process, they transformed

American politics. Never again would a campaign be run any other way."

They didn't call them spin doctors in those early days. They were advisers and managers. But now it is a proper term and quite ready to take its place in our vocabulary alongside tax audit and root canal.

Why Would Anyone Run for President?

(*Dallas Morning News,* March 11, 1999)

The question before the house, at least the houses occupied by our crowd, is why in blazes anybody would run for the presidency of the United States. Especially in these vicious times, what sort of person seeks out that sort of trouble?

Oh, there's the usual noble declaration, spoken with hand over heart and outthrust chin, of wanting to serve one's country. Text: *I want to give something back to the land that's been so good to me.* When I hear that, the first inclination is to check my hip pocket.

This question occupied the Robert W. Service Literary & Pretzel Club at a recent meeting, when we discussed why such a young turk like George W. Bush would want to paint a bull's-eye on his back and enter the presidential target range.

So, surely there are valid reasons to seek the presidency. Since this is the Age of Lists, we set down some:

• • •

You never have to admit guilt. When times are good, you can take credit. When the economy is bad, you can blame it on your predecessor or Congress.

You can go to Hawaii any time you wish.

White House room service doesn't close at midnight.

You can have James Carville deported.

No one interrupts your stories.

You never lose your car keys.

You can make chili without cleaning up the kitchen.

Nobody complains that your chili is too hot.

You don't have to carry the trash to the alley on Tuesdays and Fridays.

You can have corned beef and cabbage any night you wish.

On fishing trips, you never have to clean your catch.

You can order the surgeon general to mind his own business.

You can have your picture taken with Sophia Loren.

You never have to putt out from three feet.

You can watch any movie any time you wish, with free popcorn and real butter.

And if you have to go to the bathroom, the film is stopped until you get back.

Your mailbox is not clogged with catalogs.

If a driver cuts you off at the freeway ramp, you can put him in federal prison.

You can smoke cigars in any dang room you please.

You never have to show your driver's license to cash a check.

Or stand in line for four hours to get your driver's license renewed.

You never have to jack with the White House thermostat; there's a presidential thermostat jacker at your beck and call.

Everyone laughs at your jokes.

You don't have to worry about how much to tip.

Your barber and doctor make house calls.

Hotel clerks don't keep you waiting while carrying on telephone conversations.

You never run out of stamps.

On extended road trips, you don't have to wash your shorts in the lavatory.

Your missus never corrects you in public.

You never get a speeding ticket.

You don't have to hang up your pants at night.

If there's a button off your shirt, hey, there's a presidential seamstress on call.

You don't have to stay home from 9 to 1 o'clock, waiting for the cable repairman.

You can lie any time it's convenient.

All ladies think you're charming.

You never have to polish your shoes on the back of your pants leg.

Although it's not on the menu, the chef will make you lemonade.

You never run out of gas on the freeway.

If the party is boring, even in your own parlor, you can leave early.

Even if you never made corporal, heck, even if you were a draft dodger, you get saluted by generals.

You get $2 million severance pay. Come to think of it, go ahead, Georgie boy, we can feel your gain.

Pandora's Box Escapes Most Listeners

(*Dallas Morning News,* September 2, 1999)

In the interest of interpretive journalism, rather a fetish these days, we present a result of diligent research.

Granted, the information is old hat to highdomes who may stop off at this junction while waiting for the library to open. But this is for the common bloke, the unlettered salt of the earth. To blazes with the smarties, say we. They do not rule the land. We do, if someone will goose us on Election Day and it ain't raining. It is for the edification of the Great Unwashed that the subject of Pandora's Box is approached.

We hear the phrase repeatedly these days, mostly in connection with George W. Bush because of his early lead in the presidential marathon. Learned pundits leer at the camera and say with a condescending shrug, "Well, if the governor admits to one misdeed, he may well open Pandora's Box."

Pandora's Box was even a clue in a recent *New York Times* crossword, the epitome of recognition. Why, I remember Don January once was a *Times* crossword answer as a former PGA champion, and he wouldn't speak to commoners for weeks.

Anyways, Pandora's Box is a term used so often that the commentators, secure in their caps and gowns, assume that us bums grew up with the expression, like Mother's Day and affirmative action. Well, assume this, buster. It ain't all that well known.

• • •

The first step involved a survey of the Robert W. Service Literary & Pretzel Society at its weekly seminar. Sometime between the first and second round, the question was broached: What is this Pandora's Box we hear so dang much about?

There followed a period of reflective silence. Finally, one chap thought it was the name of an oil field over around Abilene somewheres. Another guessed it referred to a

Pentagon intern. One panelist identified Pandora's Box as the beaten favorite Sunday in the Louisiana Downs feature, and yet another remembered it as a third-down defense used by Buddy Ryan with the Bears. Two more suggested they could think better after a refill.

Finally, one fellow said he once lived upstairs over a Greek restaurant and remembered Pandora's Box as a sandwich of octopi between mulberry leaves. Actually, he came closest.

At any rate, diligent digging among research files has cleared the air and, we trust, made the political world a bit less foggy.

• • •

As astute scholars recognize, Pandora's Box came from Greek mythology. Miss Pandora was the first woman on earth, created by the god Jupiter as a gift to rival gods Prometheus and Epimetheus, whom he did not like worth a flip. In her new household, Miss Pandora discovered a secret box owned by Prometheus. In this box were kept a bunch of evils, such as revenge, envy, spite and gout and, probably, poison ivy. The world was safe from these plagues because they were locked up safely.

Curiosity got the better of Miss Pandora, and one night she sneaked to the forbidden box and peeked inside. Quickly the evils escaped and scattered over the world, where, in the manner of evils, they multiplied like rabbits.

Therefore, say the pundits, if young Master Bush admits to just one youthful misdeed, such as smoking a weed or pinching the prom queen, he may open the lid of his own Pandora's Box and a bunch of other real or imagined indiscretions will escape and flow throughout the electorate, magnifying as they go.

I offer the research, in the journalistic tradition of Joe Pulitzer and all them guys, as a public duty. Mind you, I myself lay no claims to being a scholar of the classics. As it so happened, the day we covered Greek in school, I was busy dipping Becky Thatcher's pigtails in the inkwell. Those were fun times, let me tell you.

You Were Invited, Weren't You?

(*Dallas Morning News,* January 25, 2000)

From all reports trickling down to the frontier, you and I have been assigned to a minority. We are among the few natives of our sainted Lone Star State who did not attend the inaugural doings in Washington where one of our ole pards was officially sentenced to the White House.

The structure of the inaugural festivities was the sacred project of Texans. Jeanne Johnson Phillips from our very own city orchestrated the whole shebang, just as she directed the Austin gala when our very own George W. Bush assumed the governorship. Eddie Deen from these parts drove his covered wagons north to prepare barbecue for the multitudes. David Garrido of Austin was there to do his Tex-Mex delicacies and to make sure the uninitiated furriners remove the shucks before eating the tamales. This partisan menu led Manhattan colymnist Cindy Adams to wonder vaguely what vintage champagne should be served with chili. Obviously, the lady has never tasted our state ambrosia, especially that brewed in my very own humble tepee, and until she does, my kindly counsel to her is to keep her laptop shut.

Barbra Streisand sang for the inauguration of the outgoing president, but she was nowhere to be found in our man's party. Probably her flight was canceled due to California liberalism. Instead, our Dixie Chicks offered arias from *Il Travatore,* and our Aggie troubadour Lyle Lovett, forefinger cunningly inserted in a light socket, rendered Ernest Tubb (another Texan) sonatas. Several of our famous jocks—Roger, Troy, Mack and Nolan—were there, flexing. Longhorn cattle were shipped to the Beltway, along with 9 million horses and a life-size statue of a mule. Honest to goodness.

A few loyalists missed those festivities, but with ole buster here, it was by choice. I was invited to the inaugurals, by gollies, and have the correspondence to prove it.

• • •

The invitation arrived late, but a couple of days before the events, the mailbox yielded a large envelope with the stern admonition "Do Not Bend." Obviously, the content was meant to be framed and displayed on the shanty wall. The address was beautifully hand-lettered, obviously the work of a skilled calligrapher. The return address was: Committee for The Presidential Inaugural, Washington, D.C.

Inside was an engraved parchment: *The Committee for The Presidential Inaugural requests the honor of your presence to attend and participate in the Inauguration of George Walker Bush as President of the United States of America and Richard Bruce Cheney as Vice President of the United States of America.*

Well, sir, I don't mind telling you, our little hearts went pitty-pat, and emergency calls went out to Neiman's and American Express before we noticed a second engraved sheet from the Inaugural Committee: *This invitation commemorates the inauguration* blah blah blah, and then came the stinger: *It does not constitute admission to any of the inaugural events.*

This led to a bit of puzzlement; exactly *what* were we invited to? Did you have to be invited to stand along Pennsylvania Avenue to watch the Longhorn Band march by? Did you need an official invitation to concerts in the park?

• • •

But all was not lost. Adding to the honor, there was another enclosure, an invitation to commemorate the occasion by ordering an Official 2001 Presidential Inaugural Silver Medallion, limited edition, for $195. The bronze version was a mere $48. There are inaugural coasters and a presidential memento box made of rich cherry wood ($99). How about inaugural license plates for $65?

Even though the fancy invitation denied admission to the zillion inaugural galas, there still was a certain recognition to be treasured, the exclusive opportunity to purchase certified

souvenirs from the certified inaugural committee. For some obscure reason, I was reminded of the fellow who was to be ridden out of town on a rail and said that if it weren't for the
honor of the thing, he'd just as soon walk.

Here Is One Pundit You Can Trust

(Dallas Morning News, June 1, 2000)

Way back yonder, the Good Book tells us, there were three wise men. You are constantly aware these days that the wise men have multiplied like shrimp. You can't open the newspaper or a magazine, or flick on the telly or the radio, without some learned highdome lecturing you, rather condescendingly, about everything from social morals to foreign policy to how to build a doghouse or a proper martini.

Each of these experts styles himself as a pundit, which, as Mr. Webster tells us, is a learned man who goes through life dispensing wisdom to us common lunkheads. They have distinctive names like Wolf, Cokie, Chris, Geraldo or whatever, and as far as I can determine, there ain't an ounce of frankincense or myrrh in the whole caboodle.

However, there is one pundit we can absolutely trust because he deals only in common sense. When he speaks, I pay attention.

For example, we are confused over relations with Asians, so listen to our man: "A Chinese wants to get a little piece of land, live on it, die on it and be let alone. Now, a Japanese wants to die for his country, but the Chinese is not going to let patriotism run away with his life. Life is not serious with him like it is with the Japanese. The Japanese feels he was put on earth for a purpose, but the Chinese feels he was put here by mistake."

• • •

Big business confuse you? Our adviser says, "Let Wall Street have a nightmare, and the whole country has to help get it back in bed again."

A holding company, he says, is a thing where you hand an accomplice the goods while the policeman searches you.

He could be talking about Ross Perot when he says, "Any

one of our big business men could take this country and run it fine, if he didn't have to mess with a political machine or a lot of red tape."

Plus: "The Republicans have always been the party of big business, and the Democrats of small business. The Democrats have their eyes on a dime, the Republicans on a dollar."

He has a solution for the soft-money controversy: "If we have senators and congressmen that can't protect themselves against the temptations of lobbyists, we don't need to change our lobbies, we need to change our representatives."

Shenanigans in the White House? "Nothing will spoil a big man's life like too much truth."

Plus: "Nowadays, it's about as big a crime to be dumb as it is to be dishonest."

Also: "One good thing about investigations, they always give a man a chance a second time, so he can explain how he was misunderstood the first time."

• • •

The main political parties don't confuse our man: "A Republican moves slowly. They are what we call conservatives. A conservative is a man who has plenty of money and doesn't see any reason why he shouldn't always have plenty of money. A Democrat is a fellow who never had any but doesn't see any reason why he shouldn't have some."

Also: "It's not education or training that makes a Democrat. The more education he gets, the less likely he is to be a Democrat. And if he is highly educated, he will see the applesauce in both parties."

"A Republican would naturally rather make some money under a Republican Congress, but rather than not make any at all, he'll get out and make some under the Democrats."

"A Democrat never adjourns. He is born, becomes of voting age and starts right in arguing..."

Our leader has a warning for George W. Bush when the presidential race gets cooking: "Democrats are better denouncers than the Republicans, for they have much more time to practice at it. Denouncing is not an art with the Democrats, but it's a profession."

There is infinitely more wisdom and guidance from this pundit, but it comes with a footnote. His name is Will Rogers, and he was killed in a plane crash near Anchorage, Alaska, on August 18, 1935.

Some Scams Gained Our Admiration

(*Dallas Morning News,* March 8, 2001)

To us barefoot boys with cheeks of tan, the elders were the best history teachers. Their lessons stayed snagged in memory, more so than the impersonal hieroglyphics of civic textbooks. In those days, that was our only means of research. If a dot-com had showed up, we would have fried it for supper.

Whether it be around a creek bank campfire on a winter night, while elders interpreted the bays of coondogs two pastures away, or eavesdropping on the front porch on a blistering Sunday afternoon, where the elders delivered their parables—you heard and remembered. Besides, the elders were unfettered by such bonds as editors and libel laws, and their imaginations could run free as the breeze, maybe freer.

It was in such sessions that the saga of Ma and Pa Ferguson was explored, before the Fergusons became legends and today are buried under cold calendars. They were heroes to some, scoundrels to others, but no one denied their imprint or unabashed effrontery.

• • •

Farmer Jim Ferguson was a Central Texas banker, a patron saint of tenant farmers, an avowed enemy of the Ku Klux Klan and Prohibition and apparently a devout admirer of the almighty dollar. You must realize there weren't as many of those almighty dollars around in those days, and they were treated with utmost respect.

Farmer Jim was a self-styled populist and, as such, was the successful Democratic candidate for governor in 1914. There was no middle ground; you loved him with a blind trust or you hated him as a roughshod thief. His enemies in the Legislature charged him with using state funds for personal use, and after he pledged, under oath, to repay the treasury, he reneged on his promise. So he was kicked out of the Statehouse; that is, he resigned just as impeachment set in.

A half-dozen years later, Farmer Jim tried to get on the Democratic primary ballot but was denied. So he ran his wife, Miriam A. Ferguson, whose initials immediately gained her the nickname of Ma, and he became Pa. She won but, according to the elders, was nothing but a proxy. In fact, their campaign slogan was "Two for the Price of One."

The elders, speaking without rancor, described the gubernatorial scams as many and rather crude. Pa objected to his portrayal in Texas newspapers, so he started his own, the *Ferguson Forum,* published weekly for the next 18 years. His detractors pointed out that state highway contracts seemed to be awarded to firms that advertised extensively in the *Ferguson Forum.*

• • •

Ma Ferguson served two different terms and was defeated in yet another race. There were all sorts of accusations of voter fraud in East Texas—of the Fergusons paying poll taxes for voters and padding state payrolls. The Texas Rangers supported her rival in one election, so, after she took office, she fired 33 of them. Or, rather, Pa did.

Mind you, when the elders told these stories, there was no discernible bitterness. In truth, there was some admiration attached, for those were stony times and anyone who managed to beat The System was dang near a folk hero.

The favorite scam, at least to the tellers, came about this way: If you had a relative or loved one in state prison and you wanted very much to get him out, you went across the street from the state Capitol to Pa Ferguson's private office. You would hire him as a lawyer or adviser or whatever and pay him a hefty fee. And, presto, your man would be sitting at your supper table before you could say $500, courtesy of the compassion of the humane governor. This was before—and perhaps the reason—the Board of Pardons ruled over such things.

Ma Ferguson, again according to the elders, pardoned convicts at the rate of 100 per month. In one two-year term, she issued 1,318 full and 829 conditional pardons. The elders were duly impressed that such a simple scam as selling pardons could be so successful, but, of course, those were primitive times. It could never happen today, right?

Motorists' Cell Phones Create Static

(Dallas Morning News, July 5, 2001)

It was one of those rare, dark afternoons a couple of years ago when weather gods frown upon us innocent taxpayers.

Downtown streets leading out to the hinterlands were slick with sleet and traffic that would shame a turtle. Except for the woman ahead. She was breezing along, and through her rear window, you could see her gesturing wildly with her right hand. A happy lady, undaunted by treacherous weather, keeping time to the car radio music, bless her heart.

She seemed harmless enough—that is, until you pulled alongside at the next stoplight and glanced over. The lady was still waving her right hand, but with the left, she was holding a cell phone to her ear. Wait a minute, now, she was gesturing with her right and holding a cell phone with her left? On *these* streets? What the blazes was she steering with? Had she somehow sprouted a third arm for emergencies? Was she a contortionist who could drive with her knees?

At that particular moment, exercising my rights under the Constitution, I voted against hand-held cell phones in automobiles. In my mind, anyway.

Of course, honesty compels me to admit a prejudice against telephones of any ilk, mainly because when one of the blamed things rings, I say 8-5 it's bad news. And if I am due bad news, I prefer it came by slower methods, by the whim of the Postal Service maybe or, even better, smoke signals.

But that is hardly democratic. One supposes, under the Bill of Rights, if a citizen wishes to spend a goodly part of his day on the phone, it's his—excuse the expression—funeral. Driving in scatterbrained traffic is hazardous enough, without some chatterbox occupying half of your concentration with news about Rosemary's baby, but it's your choice. Except, like with the icy street lady, when it's my physical welfare you're jacking with.

At any rate, the car-cell-phone ban is coming, sure as little green apples. New York State already has outlawed the thing, starting this fall. You still may have a cell phone, but it must be a headset or some contraption that doesn't require use of a hand. Other states will surely follow.

The opposition will come from folks who object to further government control of anything, any increase in the Big Brother premise. (Big Brother was the all-controlling government in the George Orwell satire 1984, written in 1949 and predicting the eventual clamp The Party will have on every facet of serfdom.)

· · ·

Normally, we grizzled independents would oppose any increase in government dictatorial power. Like putting cameras on stoplights to nail drivers who run the yellow and red lights. Fifty cities have installed these spies and are sacking literally millions of extra dollars in traffic fines.

So we need not worry about cell phones signaling some sort of government takeover. Big Brother, if you think about it, is already here, ruling the most minute facets of existence. Almost everywhere you go—department stores, convenience stores, hotel corridors, even on city streets—surveillance cameras track your moves.

Big Brother tells us when and where and if we can smoke, how many fish we can catch and what size. He has a record of every phone call you make. Recently, we learned that some rental car agencies have a monitor on their vehicles to record speeds, so that fines may be assessed if you secretly break the limit. BB specifies the material of garbage bags we use for pickups and when and where. If they choose, government gumshoes can park a van two blocks away, aim magic rays through your walls and tell how many spoons of sugar you put on your oatmeal.

So let us not furrow our noble foreheads about a cell phone

POLITICS AND GOVERNMENT

ban signaling the arrival of Big Brother. He is already here, sitting on your couch, controlling your thermostat, occasionally raiding the icebox and specifying exactly how much water can be used to flush your commode, for goodness sakes, and he's not even a tax write-off.

Pretty Soon, You're Talking About Real Money

(Dallas Morning News, January 31, 2002)

The problem is, the day they covered trigonometry and cosines and high finance in school, most of us commoners were out with the whooping cough. We passed up the Wharton School of Business because it had no football team.

As a consequence, the Great Unwashed has serious problems with zeros. We can go as high as a thousand dollars or possibly a million, but any higher amount makes our eyes cross. National budgetary folk speak in unknown tongues. They throw in words like *billion* and *trillion* with the casualness of Rusty Greer playing catch, and we no more get the picture than a hog knows it's Sunday.

We have tried mightily to understand this Enron collapse— what skulduggery the big shots pulled off, the shell companies, the offshore accounts, the false loans and the stock unloads— and we have wound up with a severe pain behind the eyes.

• • •

Mostly, perhaps cynically, we think this: A mug can stick up a neighborhood bank, get road-blocked on the freeway and spend the next 20 birthdays making little rocks out of big ones. But the Enron bigwigs, with the exception of a couple of sacrificial underlings, will walk free as the breeze or maybe freer. Oh, Kenneth Lay may have to sell one of his palatial estates in Aspen, but he won't do a day in the slammer. They'll argue this case, trading blame back and forth, until kingdom come. Remember, like the two hippies explaining their housekeeping: just keep kicking the trash around the floor until it disappears.

Two generations of attorneys will earn enough fees to retire to the south of France. The feds will spend untold millions and the same number of manpower hours investigating. Last we heard, there were four different government outfits launching probes. I think that is the way they put it—launching probes. We could cure cancer with the money the government will spend on this Enron tangle. If this be street-corner cynicism, so be it.

• • •

Of course, us common taxpayers are punch-drunk by now. Hit us another lick, we're numb. We heard a fellow say the other day that this war on terrorism and its far-flung repercussions are costing us—you and me—$1 billion a day. Can this be true? Let's see, there are how many zeros in a billion? And we haven't even started repairing the damage our own bombs caused in Afghanistan. That's supposed to cost us $296 million the first year. By the way, how much does a 2,000-pound bomb cost, and how about those 15,000-pound "daisy cutters"? They gotta go around ten grand each, don't they? How many did we drop?

Let's see now, in the immediate Sept. 11 aftermath, the president whipped off $5 billion cash to the airlines and went on tab for another $10 billion because their business had suffered. There was $20 billion shipped to New York. Congress approved another $40 billion for military operations, anti-terrorism and disaster relief. The president wants to increase military spending by $48 billion next year, up to $379 billion. That's *billion,* dear hearts. Tom Ridge wants to double the anti-terrorism budget, to $37.7 billion. Just out of pocket change, we flip $100 million in military aid to the Philippines. Hand me more naughts, son, fore I tan yore hide.

It's enough to make the common guy wonder: Where in the blazes is all this dough coming from? We're not questioning the expenditures, for that might seem unpatriotic. But we hear all these unfathomable amounts, and we just stand there looking dizzy and silly.

The intelligence folk tell us that the original purpose of Osama bin Laden's September doings was to hit Uncle Sam in the pocketbook. If that is so, you must admit he was successful.

We don't yet have President Bush's new budget. Some smarts say it's going to run around two trillion. How much is a trillion anyway? Perhaps it behooves us unlettered taxpayers to hope and trust, perhaps blindly, that we don't run out of zeros.

When Politicians Start Speaking in Tongues, Duck

(*Dallas Morning News,* September 8, 2001)

The trouble, with you and me and the guy on the next stool, is that we don't know what the tomfool they are talking about. The language of Our Fathers Who Art in Washington is from another planet. Jabberwocky, they call it. Can you imagine the Gettysburg Address in current Beltway nomenclature? Eyes would cross before the second sentence.

It is not only Washspeak that is foreign to common folk. The new business community also delights in unknown tongues. Example: Recently arriving at this desk was a company communique outlining goals for the new year: "Begin monetizing the user database. Complete the gold standard roll-out and optimize our content costs." Now, you show me a person who understands that, and I will show you a person I do not wish to spend a lot of time with, unless I am trying to fall asleep. The language has passed us little people by.

A pessimistic soul might suspect government authors of a confusion conspiracy, calculated to make the average Joe give up trying to understand, write another check for taxes and trust the fellows he voted for To Do the Right Thing.

Just off the top of the common head, President Bush's ambition to remodel the country's defense system seems a progressive idea. And if this means a drastic reorganization and merger of the Navy, Marines, Army and Air Force, then so be it. Put all the forces under one hat and eliminate piles of paperwork and manpower duplication. Maybe we could optimize our content costs, whatever the heck that means.

• • •

The next war, perish the thought, won't be waged with heavy cruisers and hand grenades any more than World War II was fought with flintlocks. But if you quit spending zillions on certain aircraft, even if same are outmoded the moment they roll off the assembly line, you are shutting down plants that employ thousands. How do you think the senators from the particular state are going to react? You would hope they would place the country's interest above their state's welfare, but you dassn't bet on it.

There has been a study called RMA ("Revolution in Military Affairs") under way for a decade or so, and you sense that President Bush and Defense Secretary Donald Rumsfeld would dearly love to see it implemented. Of course, the RMA has its own modern language, such as "info dominance," "asymmetric competitor" and—get this—"deep-strike architecture," which scares the pants off you and me. But it is based on the space age, on such contraptions as a bomber that could fly 60 miles high, drop a precision missile down a smokestack halfway around the world and be home in time for supper. It's spooky to think about, but, then, so was the A-bomb. You remember old Fat Boy, outmoded today as the rub board.

• • •

Apparently, the RMA would close many military camps and posts (which bring significant money into their communities) and use those funds to help do its Star War thing. The traditional military, its generals and admirals, surely will fight the idea with their considerable muscle. And it would ruffle feathers in Russia and China, which then would feel obligated to keep up.

It all is gobbledygook for The Great Unwashed, who can only hope that common sense will prevail. And common sense tells you that the big guys don't want to get mixed up in an actual missile war that could obliterate a country before sundown. The little guys, ah, there's the rub.

While our leaders are up there in space with Buck Rogers contraptions and their own unique language, we hope no one overlooks the kook who gets on a southbound bus in Montreal, with a suitcase full of some formula he whipped up

POLITICS AND GOVERNMENT

in his garage, and gives diphtheria to every soul in Philadelphia. Or another who steals a fast pickup, loads up with homemade fire bombs, drives through the dry woodlands of California and costs the government 18 zillion billion dollars it might otherwise spend on missiles. Say, there's a thought.

The Media

Fourth Estate Follies and Fortes

Memories Are Made of This

(*Dallas Times Herald,* June 2, 1975)

Presley T. Ervin could not sleep late. Maybe it was guilty conscience, as we always claimed, but more likely it was the arthritis pains that gnarled his hands and stiffened his knees. Presley T. was called Puss Ervin by all, and at five ayem, he would be found at his desk in the old hot, dirty Fort Worth Press, pecking out his bowling column for the day. His shirt would be thrown across a chair and his work costume was a speckled BVD top, in protest of the woefully inadequate air conditioning system even at that early hour. The specks were result of frequent eruptions by the overhead ventilator, which would belch and throw a horrible shower of soot on victims below. This would always be greeted with a great burst of oaths from Presley T. Ervin, who claimed he learned his colorful language while "kicking boots" at Great Lakes Naval Training Center during World War I.

Presley T. was old as a tree or maybe older and he wore a pair of baggy pants that looked as if a band of gypsies had just moved out of the seat. His winter garment was an old Chicago Cub warmup jacket, a memo of the days when he served as a bird dog for same. Puss was a retired postman whose great delight was in sneaking up on young sportswriters and giving them a fearful frog on their biceps. He also was not adverse to taking a slug of warm gin from a bottle he kept under the front seat of his old Ford.

• • •

Puss Ervin was just one of a rather unorthodox procession of sportswriters who stopped off at the *Fort Worth Press* during the ten lean years I spent thereabouts. The place seemed to attract individualists; there was no conformity as we highly organized journalists know today. The *Press* was too small and bony, for one thing. It was so small, can you believe this, that it didn't even have a vice-president.

The *Press* paid comparable wages to the establishment *Star-Telegram,* but there was no operating capital, no travel budget, no expense funds, too few staff members. Perhaps for that matter, the editors let young writers set their own guidelines, find their own groove and rhythm.

They spent a lot of time snickering. Almost daily there would be a 50-yard dash down the wide sidewalk, the loser to buy the coffee at the nearby White Way Café. Occasionally there would be a standing broad jump contest on the lawn of the county health center across the street, which always resulted in a zillion pens and pencils flying from Presley T. Ervin's shirt pocket and hiding themselves in the grass.

Someone discovered that a support for the only stall in the men's room made an ideal chinning bar. So each morning, after the first deadline, the six members of the sports department would troop through the city room to the men's restroom for a chinning contest. The sourpots around the copy desk would glance sardonically at each other, wondering what the tomfool those crazy jerks would do next.

Of course, no department was clean of weirdos. That same copydesk, for example, once had a rim man, name long forgotten, whose lunch always consisted solely of carrots, each bite of which he would chew exactly 88 times. Then he would use a rubber band for dental floss. He sometimes stretched a rope from the copy desk to a pillar and demonstrated his tightrope walking, which he claimed was excellent for the heart and lungs. When he was fired in one of those periodical economic pinches, he bore no malice. He bought a tiny apple farm near Sacramento, planned to convert to carrots and—like Yossarian in Catch-22—fully intended to live forever or die in the attempt.

Dan Jenkins, who came to work for the *Press* fresh from Paschal High, was frightened witless by snakes. We conducted a continual search for color pictures of snakes; we would trim them carefully and roll them in Jenkins' typewriter so when he arrived early in the ayem, smoking a Camel and drinking a Coke, Jenkins would put a sheet of copy paper in his typewriter, twirl the carriage and out would roll this horrible rattlesnake. He would give a brief shout of dismay before getting wearily to work. Even now, at his desk at *Sports Illustrated* in New York, Jenkins occasionally opens a letter and a snake picture falls out and he shakes for a while.

There was the great Watergun Caper, in which Jerre R. Todd (whom we called Spanky The Child Star) drove a delivery boy batty. The lad made hourly deliveries of engravings to the composing room, then he would pause a short distance away to read the latest news flashes on the UPI teletype. Todd would give him a short spurt on the back of the neck with his watergun and, of course, everybody would dummy up when he wheeled to investigate. The kid complained continually that the roof leaked, even in clear weather. One day when the boy left the building in bright sunshine, Todd leaned out a second-story window and popped him with a long burst. The lad never even looked up; he broke into a high gallop and we never saw him again.

• • •

Sick Charley Modesette was the sports deskman and he loved to have a few beers and play the honkytonk piano. Sick Charley was the only guy ever known to beat Hodgkins Disease. He was working for a New Mexico paper when he was so diagnosed. The paper sent him to New York for last-ditch treatment, and Charley said he got rather discouraged when he got on the plane and found they had bought him a one-way ticket. Charley beat Hodgkins but he darn near didn't survive a handball game at the YMCA. He had a heart attack during a game, and Spanky The Child Star, somehow getting his first aid lessons confused, leaped on Sick Charley and started pumping his chest in artificial respiration. Sick Charley somehow made it through the crisis, but his wife never forgave Spanky and small wonder.

It was a time of learning and laughing. We read Lardner,

Perelman and Thurber and Runyon and Max Schulman and tried, quite unabashedly, to steal their styles. The freedom was rather wonderful, and it must have worked on some. Jenkins has authored two best-selling novels which have established him as maybe the foremost sports satirist of our time. Bud Shrake went on to become a prolific novelist, a fine serious writer who also has done highly praised film work. Gary Cartwright also graduated into novels and film writing. Julian Read became one of the state's leading political public relations men. Todd has his own advertising agency in Fort Worth. Sick Charley and Presley T. Ervin lived to ripe old terms before cashing out. Andy Anderson was the only one of the old crew still aboard when the *Press* sank last week. The poor thing had never been a profitable operation; some called it a scandal sheet, others a Mickey Mouse newspaper. But the freedom and spirit thereabouts was a rare training track, and many of us are indeed grateful for its laps.

Spiro Agnew Nailed Us Natterers

(Dallas Morning News, October 3, 1996)

You must say this for the late Spiro Agnew. He sent many fellow citizens to the friendly neighborhood dictionary.

The fellow's most remembered quote—perhaps his *only* remembered quote—resurfaced recently when the former vice president bought the farm.

"Nattering nabobs of negativism," he once called us esteemed members of the Froth Estate and assorted "intellectuals."

Mostly, it was "nattering" that caused momentary confusion. It is not a word bantered about your ordinary breakfast table.

Some placed nattering as a special weave found only in Neiman Marcus tweed jackets. Others thought it referred to a Seminole method to fry goggle-eyed perch. Of course, we learned semanticists knew immediately that Mr. Agnew was using a British term for complaining or grumbling. "Nabob" we knocked off as a person who gains power in India or other Eastern countries. Negativism, of course, is another name for one of those things sticking up from a car battery.

Actually, Mr. Agnew was describing the media as a surly mob of egotistical boobs who sought a snake in every woodpile.

The vice president received considerable attention for his terminology. In those days, it was a rare condemnation from such high office. Privately, most political bigwigs wouldn't spit in a newspaperman's face if his moustache was on fire. But they were wary of antagonizing us nabobs.

"Never pick a fight with a man who buys ink by the barrel" is a famous old directive from Niccolo Machiavelli or former Sen. Gary Hart.

• • •

Of course, Mr. Agnew worked for Richard Nixon, who

tried, without total success, to mask his disdain for the press. The vice president didn't bother to disguise his feelings. Mr. Agnew also had a speech writer named Pat Buchanan, who apparently loved to tweak the media, even though he later became a prominent member of same.

You can sense some ambitious speech writer, all caught up in alliteration, putting words in the Agnew mouth. "Hopeless, hysterical hypochondriacs of history" was another fancy phrase. Come on, fellows, nobody talks like that, not even a vice president.

At any rate, filtering the Agnew words through the gauze of years, we must admit he was uncomfortably close to being correct. The media, as a whole, does seem to accentuate the negative. We tend to be a-ginners who feel it is more blessed to accuse than defend. There was a recent reference in the *New Yorker* magazine: "the fog of TV sound bites and media sleaze which hangs over America like a low static cloud, shutting out the sunlight and blurring all the stars."

Of course, The Great Unwashed must share the blame. The sleaze is there because it sells. The public, while condemning the messenger, slobbers over the message.

Example: Johnnie Hernandez and Joseph McCoy were both Dallas cops in the news about the same time. Mr. Hernandez was the policeman involved in the Michael Irvin case, the one doing time right now. Mr. McCoy was an off-duty cop who jumped in a swimming pool, pulled a child out and administered CPR. Saved a life. Which do you remember?

• • •

The Agnew mistake, as some of us claim, was to lump all media together and tar the whole wad with the same brush. About the same time, from the floor of the Senate, Barry Goldwater looked up at the press gallery and said, "You are a rotten bunch." He didn't say three-fourths of you are a rotten bunch, or one-half. The brand was all-encompassing.

The same tactic is used by those who employ a currently popular classification. Ross Perot constantly refers to "the liberal press" as if *all* media are liberal. Without exception. Rush Limbaugh and his strident tribe do the same.

This, of course, is a bum rap. There is a media segment that perhaps should be classified as conservative. Further, there is a segment striving to be completely fair and honorable, neither conservative nor liberal. But, regretfully, there is something we can't deny. We are natterers all.

Gypsy May Be in Soul,
But Not in Newsroom

(Dallas Morning News, February 11, 1999)

The name has faded from memory, but the fellow was in his 40s, wore suspenders and smoked a pipe. Goodness, how he smoked that dang pipe while pecking at the old L.C. Smith typewriter. He was constantly lighting the thing with wooden matches, from a large grocery matchbox in his desk drawer.

The publisher of the small Texas newspaper fancied himself William Randolph Hearst and was not a favorite of the staff. With the exception of the pipe smoker, we all were painfully young and impetuous. One night, after the boss called in some irritating order, the young reporters stomped around the newsroom, voicing threats of various nature. Quitting on the spot. Arson. Sending anonymous notes to the publisher's wife. The pipe smoker said nothing.

"And you," barked a whipper-snapper, "what're you going to do about it?"

The guy removed the pipe from its pier. "Well, I got a full box of matches here," he said. "No sense wasting 'em."

One night a few weeks later, the reporter tamped his pipe and reached for a match. He shook the box and there was no sound. With never a word, he arose, clapped on his hat and stalked out, never to be seen again in those parts.

● ● ●

That was our first exposure to a legendary figure—the itinerant newspaperman, whose tribe was becoming extinct. These guys were as much a part of print history as the linotype and the rotary press. They floated from town to town, job to job, writing, quite competently, on any subject from a county road contract to a semi-pro-baseball game. They lived in seedy rooming houses, at the greasy spoon and frequently showed up at the pool hall with a pint of Mint Springs. After sufficient nips, they might recite from *King Lear,* and more likely than not, they knew all the words to *The Cremation of Sam McGee.*

They were restless loners. You might find a Samuel Clemens among them or a William Sydney Porter or a Damon Runyon. More likely, they were faceless nomads, eyes fixed on the horizon like scouts searching for a new campsite near firewood and water. They were a part of reportorial civilization, now gone from the wind.

A significant hint of their passing, to me anyway, came a few years later when a Fort Worth editor and I interviewed a job applicant from another city.

"What about your retirement plan?" he asked. The editor and I exchanged blank looks. He might as well have been asking the sexual practices of the duckbill platypus. Retirement plan? Pension? You mean those things that postmen and railroad engineers get?

But of such benefits, newspaper roots eventually were born. Soon, reporters were family men, had 2.3 children, hurried home to mow lawns and sang tenor in the Rotary Club chorus.

• • •

This void in The Human Comedy came to mind recently when a geezer named Ted Marchibroda was fired as coach of the Baltimore Ravens. The notion suddenly struck that coaches and managers have replaced the itinerant newspaperman.

Mentioned in the Marchibroda story was the fact that he had held 10 jobs, assistant and boss, in his 34 terms in the pro leagues. Actually, that seems about average. Bill Parcells, the Jets coach, has worked 12 jobs in his 32 years. Marv Levy wore 13 hats before he sought the couch.

And they are the fortunate few who got head jobs. Assistants are the true migrants. One Dallas Cowboy assistant, Jim Bates, has his 14th address in 28 seasons. Another, Dwain Painter, also has made 14 stops, and he'll be 57 next week.

143

Baseball assistants? Forget it. They don't even have tepees. They live out of station wagons.

In retrospect, I don't regret missing the gypsy life. Once I stayed at one newspaper for 26 years. When I left for another post, a TV interviewer asked why.

"Wanderlust, probably," I said, rather wittily it seemed to me.

Public Gets the News It Wants

(Dallas Morning News, June 8, 2000)

The president was very angry. He complained bitterly that the press was printing lies about his administration and attempting to smear almost everything he was attempting.

Attacks by journalists, he said, were "outrages on common decency." He told associates that if disregard for "truth and fairness" and "willful and malignant representation" continued, it might become nearly impossible to govern the country.

The president was George Washington, back when menfolks wore knickers and wigs. I dug out this old story recently after hearing a Jesse Ventura interview. Some goldythroat asked the Minnesota governor what he thought about George W. Bush.

"I like the fellow," said the rassler. "We've hung out together at governors' meetings, and we have some things in common."

What?

"Well, for one thing, we both hate the media."

Hey, wait a minute. Gov. Bush hates the media?

"That's what he told me."

In his latest book, Gov. Ventura describes reporters as corrupt, shameless and irresponsible. In all probability, the governor's contemporaries locked themselves in their soundproof sanctums and applauded.

The point of these stories is that nothing has changed and that politicians' distrust of the media didn't just get off the bus. But, as some sage said, "Every time history repeats itself, the price goes up."

• • •

The stories support another old habit—that Washington, Gov. Ventura, Gov. Bush, whoever, all lump the media together under a general classification. We're all bums, better branded with an "M" on our sloping foreheads and banished to Molokai.

Say a survey find that 95 percent of the Beltway press corps is liberal; ergo, 95 percent of the entire nation's press is liberal. Trust me, this simply is not true. There is a diversification among the media, just as there is in Congress, but that premise is a tough sell. Most folks in the media finally shrug and accept the brand.

It's more likely that most political coverage seems "anti" because it's easier to drum up a story that way. Remember, Spiro Agnew tagged us "nattering nabobs of negativism."

Despite their stigma, apparently the media rascals still carry some weight, even though they are cursed by lord and knave alike.

At a recent media panel at the University of Michigan, the consensus was that the media has a telling effect on warfare.

"If the media is against a war," said President Gerald Ford, "it's impossible for the government to go on with it."

"Vietnam was the first war on television," said journalist James Cannon. "And it showed the people at home that war was so grisly, I don't think people will ever support another war." (If that theory is valid, perhaps the media is not such a no-good bum after all.)

Is there too much mistrust by the media?

"When I was a kid," said commentator Bernard Kalb, "when the government said something, the press didn't hold it up to the light. Now these days, everything is examined."

Historian Haynes Johnson agreed, "George Washington went to his grave despising the press. So did Thomas Jefferson and John Adams. And they weren't living when every minutiae is examined every day."

• • •

Despite the politicians' dislike and distrust of the press, the media business will endure. Raymond Chandler once said, "A newspaper is a business out to make money through advertising revenue. That is predicated on its circulation, and you know what circulation depends on."

Take that premise and multiply it by scads of televisions and radios and magazines and the Internet, and you have an overpowering force, even if some politicos consider it an evil force.

As for the reporters and commentators themselves, they may be a no-win proposition. As was the eager war correspondent at Gettysburg, determined to establish his impartiality to both sides. So he donned trousers of Confederate gray and a tunic of Union blue. And the Johnny Rebs shot him in the chest, while the Union soldiers shot him in the seat.

Our Age of Media Overkill

(*Dallas Morning News,* May 11, 2000)

You have heard it many times of late. The remark usually is preceded by a furtive look over each shoulder and lowering the voice as if you were in a strange church and asking a pew neighbor for directions to the men's room. You're not quite sure how the words will be received, but there they are anyway.

"I'm damn tired of hearing about that Cuban kid."

Not even waiting for a response, the speaker quickly begins a new discourse, thereby allowing his audience a chance to remain noncommittal. So there, I'm on record, and I'm glad I got it off my chest; now, what were you saying about Dennis Rodman?

The adventures of young Elián González and his kinfolk and his father and Janet Reno and Fidel Castro and Al Gore and Tom DeLay and Trent Lott and a cast of howling masses on both sides have been detailed in print, in voice, in film, over and over and over like an old 78 rpm with a snagged needle.

Once again we would have grumbled in private, but then came the sordid invasion of politics and the fierce intrusion of outsiders in hopes of sharing the spotlight. Even a cool fish like Hillary Clinton has decried the "political exploitation and the incredible media circus." And, you must admit, Mrs. Clinton has had every opportunity to learn both fields.

Most of us seem to wish, however furtively, that all this static would fade and the kid could go back to being a kid and we may all live happily ever after. Or at least until the next media crisis arrives or is manufactured.

• • •

When historians get around to naming this era, like the Great Depression or the Boomer Generation, these days may well be labeled the Birth of Media Overkill. When scientists of the far future discover our bones, they will wonder at the over-sized eardrums and the fingers curved to fit around—what is that thing?—oh, a remote tuner.

There was this uneasy feeling back in 1997, when Princess Diana died in that horrible Paris auto smash, that the coverage was just a bit much. It wasn't a continuing saga—like the O.J. Simpson murder trial. The Diana coverage became the same words and the same tragic scene and the same camera focus on the same piled flowers. But we didn't complain then about excess coverage, not out loud anyway. It didn't seem proper or respectful.

Then came the John Kennedy Jr. airplane disappearance and the resulting scramble for new angles, Kennedy friends to flush out and interviews with any pilot who could tell a biplane from a Greyhound bus. This time, there was a faint rumble of protest against continued over-and-over-and-over wordage from reporters assigned to, excuse the expression, the death watch. But, as the Brits say, it didn't seem "good form" to complain.

• • •

Now, however, with the Elián González thing, the media finds its ranks swelled manyfold. Not only the basic networks but all the news channels and cable networks and dot.coms and whatever else are cluttering our ozone. How many times have you seen the boy playing on the backyard swing? A zillion? Two zillion?

Some curmudgeons saw this massive media gathering in Little Havana as buzzards circling a desert carrion. Seeing this collection of cameras and microphones and note pads, the politicians couldn't resist. And it was these politicians and their clutching at the spotlight that soured The Great Unwashed and led some to grumble, however carefully.

There will be other opportunities on other stories in the future. Overkill is with us to stay; there doesn't seem to be any way to reduce same.

However, at the other extreme is government control of the press, as in many countries. Or a newspaper office bombed or

THE MEDIA

a radio commentator gunned down in his driveway. Within the last fortnight, in Iran, 16 reform newspapers were shut down by the government, leaving just seven dailies in the land.

The media may be considered like rainfall. There's either too much or too little.

Media Badge or a Sign of Contempt?

(Dallas Morning News, March 1, 2001)

Were it not for these large pointy ears, long legs and bushy tail, you would never mistake us for a small omnivorous canid of Africa and Asia. But transport us into the Minnesota snowdrifts and you may immediately identify my tribe as jackals.

It's about the lowest term you can bestow on us sedate, dignified gentlemen. Worse than a polecat or cottonmouth water moccasin. Jackals slink up after braver animals have slain the supper, then dine off the leavings, keeping a wary eye cocked for the cops.

In large areas of the political hemisphere, jackals are portrayed by The Media. That's according to Minnesota's foremost blowhard.

Gov. Jesse Ventura, former rassler and professional showboat, has never masked his contempt for The Media, and now he has made it a matter of record. The governor has issued media credentials labeled "Official Jackal" and decreed that reporters dealing with him must wear these credentials around their scrawny little necks.

Lettering on the Official Jackal card warns the reporter that the governor reserves the right to revoke this credential for any reason. Further, reads the large print, "This credential DOES NOT include parking privilege." Now, really.

Several states require special identifications for reporters, but it is the jackal label that ruffles some news organizations. The *St. Paul Pioneer Press* returned the credentials in a proper huff. The Associated Press instructed its reporters not to wear same, saying, "It may be intended to demean them and their profession."

• • •

The governor's press secretary said, "The jackal is a joke. The line gives us the right to control the actual use or abuse of the credential. If you read anything more into this, you're being paranoid."

Well, of course, us sedate media gentlemen reserve the right to be paranoid if we so wish. Says so right in the Bill of Rights.

The nomenclature comes from the title of Gov. Ventura's book, *Going To the Mat Against Political Pawns and Media Jackals.*

Further, the governor will tell you, his disdain for the media is shared by officeholders everywhere. He once mentioned that he discovered at governors' confabs that he and George W. Bush had one thing in common: They both hated the media.

Of course, us old typewriter rascals like to think we are excluded from the jackal pack, that the media these days includes far more than ink-stained wretches and that anyone who owns a tape recorder or a computer now claims membership in The Fourth Estate, although they wouldn't know a linotype from a stagecoach. Further, we say, the new crowd has difficulty separating fact from opinion and wouldn't recognize a scruple if it bit them on the thumb.

However, we fool ourselves. We have long been classified as jackals or very near, even when reporting was limited to quill and foolscap.

From Bob Dole's book *Great Political Wit:* "At one point during his long political career, Thomas Jefferson became so angry over press attacks that he suggested that newspapers should be divided into four sections: (1) Truth, (2) Probability, (3) Possibility, (4) Lies."

• • •

You wonder perhaps if Gov. Ventura is a bit smarter than your average rock. With his theatrical background, the chap knew he would be the media butt, that pundits would delight in stressing his blundering and that cartoonists and squawk shows would depict him as a bargain basement buffoon. So he beat them to it. A vicious offense is the best defense.

The governor has a sideline, you know. He is the chief TV commentator for this new football league started by his old rassle promoter Vince McMahon. The XFL was greeted with great glee by pressboxers the land over. It was a perfect target for wisecracks.

So before one recent game, Gov. Ventura sounded off on camera.

"How about all these smart aleck newspaper guys writing sarcastic things about our league?" roared the governor. "I call 'em pukes! Not one ever strapped on a helmet! Pukes!"

Maybe now we have a choice of classification: jackals or pukes. This may take some thought.

Writers and Filmmakers

Purveyors of Inspiration and Sometimes Perspiration

Thurber's Sly Works Hold Up Well

(*Dallas Morning News,* August 25, 1994)

A casual thumbing of the daily blat last week caused a sharp pang of conscience. In one way, this came as a relief because I hadn't realized the dang thing was still operative. However, default kicked in when a story from Ohio reminded that James Thurber, were he alive, would be 100 years old.

The conscience twanged with realization it had been months since I had reread some Thurber. He was my first and remains my foremost American literary icon, and to neglect him for any measurable period is unforgivable, like failing to call home on Mother's Day.

Mr. Thurber is loosely classified as an essayist, but essay is a foreboding word; it sounds like something your ninth-grade English teacher told you to have ready by Friday and you hated it. Whatever Mr. Thurber wrote was short and simple yet finely crafted as an Incan aqueduct. The intrigue was not in his topics but in his sly handling of same. There was no crash, bang, whack to his verbs. Eventually the reader realized he was being rendered helpless by gentle whops with a satirical pillow.

All this, despite physical handicaps; he lost an eye in a childhood accident, and sight gradually failed in the other. For much of his life, he drew his wonderful cartoons with the visual boost of something called a Zeiss loop. His pieces, mostly for the *New Yorker,* were composed almost as laboriously.

• • •

In my favorite Thurber story, he referred to his faulty sight with characteristic wryness.

During World War I, young Mr. Thurber was regularly called before the Columbus draft board for physical examination. He was disqualified on his first visit, but for some reason, his exemption never made it into the permanent files, and he would be summoned again in a fortnight.

Always he would get as far as the eye doctor, who would give him an accusing stare: "Why, you have no business here with sight like that!"

Young Mr. Thurber tired of explaining, so he would return home and patiently await another draft summons and hear the same dismissal. He became a familiar yet unidentified figure around the draft offices.

One day, idly awaiting his turn to be probed, he picked up an unemployed stethoscope and affixed it to his ears out of curiosity. A physician hurried by and called, "Would you mind giving us a hand over here, doctor? We're a bit rushed."

Before he realized it, Mr. Thurber was examining draftees, applying his stethoscope to various chests and nodding wisely. In those days—as I suppose would happen now—some fellows were adverse to military service and would do almost anything to escape same. (This, of course, was before Canada was discovered.)

One youth, in desperation to fail the physical, swallowed his watch.

Mr. Thurber applied his stethoscope, became extremely puzzled and called an elderly doctor for consultation. This examiner listened intently, moving his stethoscope around. Then, removing his ear pieces, he affixed the youth with a penetrating glare.

"My good man," he said. "You seemed to have swallowed a watch."

The fellow, of course, was highly embarrassed. *"On purpose?"* he cried.

"I presume," said the doctor, "that you'd be the best judge of that."

• • •

Probably the world, if it bothers, remembers Mr. Thurber best for his classic *The Secret Life of Walter Mitty*. But he has countless others. The first Thurber piece I ever read was *What Do You Mean It Was Brillig?*, and I was hopelessly addicted.

He wrote fables and foibles and folderol. He wrote a masterful fairy tale called *The Wonderful World of O,* in which cruel pirates captured an island and outlawed the letter O, as in hope and love and valor. Books became bks, and coats became cats. Until a day when a magical force prevailed, and the O's attacked. There were onslaughts by owls and crows and loons and woodcocks and frogs and toads and locusts, and in the woods, roads were clogged with toadstools and mushrooms and wolfbane and bloodroot and on and on, until the world was OK once more.

Critics often braced Mr. Thurber with the ancient whine: Why didn't he write a novel? It was not a question he fancied.

"Is a miniaturist any less artist than someone who paints a mural?" he demanded and, in my mind anyway, wheeled and stalked away in a proper huff.

Scribblers Rode Pens a Long Way

(*Dallas Morning News,* April 13, 2000)

A century or so ago, there was a wry chap who ran the YMCA gym in a Central Texas town named Harley Davidson Mitchell. The fellow, not the town. His daddy was the local motorcycle dealer. True story.

Years after our acquaintance lapsed and various projects for the government and assorted newspapers had taken me to far reaches, there came a communiqué from the old friend.

"Unlike you, I have not been around the world," he wrote. "However, I have traveled extensively in Bell County."

That's precisely my sentiment this week as a particular product arrived at bookstores, a novel titled *The Borderland.* And it leads to a steal of Mr. Harley Davidson Mitchell's resume.

I have never been a novelist, but I have knew some.

This particular novelist I have knew is titled Edwin Shrake, and he has been spouting these literary geysers for, oh, maybe four decades now, off and on. I suppose you could call this his Big Work, although he ain't done no dogs.

The first one was titled *Blood Reckoning,* and I vividly recall the day he sold same. The mail brought a publisher's check for $3,000, which he promptly traded for a used white Cadillac about the size of the courthouse, which made him a respected book author in our crowd, especially since the thing would occasionally start without a booster cable. We bystanders thought the novel was pretty dang good, but it was difficult to separate literary assessment from personal bias, especially since the latter afforded occasional rides in the white Cadillac when we could get the dang thang started.

• • •

There was another early Shrake novel named *Blessed McGill* that we judged vastly underrated, even if the white

Cadillac had already gone to That Great Junkyard In The Sky. Much, much later, Mr. Shrake happened to co-host a little golf volume with famed teacher Harvey Penick, which became the biggest selling sports book of all time. All time!

Now here is *The Borderland,* a product of about 30 years of research and procrastination of various grades. The story sets in that awkward Texas phase between the Alamo and statehood. But the novel, like Herman Wouk's *Winds of War,* feeds you history in painless doses. While you are absorbed in Sam Houston's feud with the grasping Mirabeau Lamar and his shameless betrayal of the Comanche and Cherokee tribes, there is enough shooting and bleeding and rooting around to mask the history.

But, admittedly, this review is from a prejudiced source. Someone else will have to put the calipers to this one.

Bud Shrake comes from that remarkable pod of writers hatched on a threadbare little newspaper in Fort Worth, three youngsters who honed their claws as unfettered pressboxers, who went to bed each night clutching Hemingway volumes like teddy bears. Dan Jenkins, of course, has spouted novels at regular intervals, *Semi-Tough* and all those tales of Billy Clyde Puckett and them, plus other football and golf novels, selling same to movies for enough money to buy goodly portion of Florida beachfront, which he did for a time.

The third of that improbable little clutch, Gary Cartwright, majored in nonfiction, although he had a hockey novel that some of us considered top drawer.

• • •

After flings in various climes, the three pals returned to semi-roots, Mr. Shrake and Mr. Cartwright to Austin and Mr. Jenkins to Fort Worth, where they continue to grind it out.

I am continually boggled by the quantity and quality of their products, although admittedly it is from a prejudiced boggle station. All together, the trio has written 18 novels and 17 nonfiction books and a dozen movies and television plays and approximately 2 million and three magazine pieces. Join

161

me in finding this rather amazing, all springing from one scruffy little nest.

Of course, I could have done the same and would have if my back hadn't hurt so much and, besides, somebody had to stay home and mind the store.

Experience Didn't Batter This Poet

(*Dallas Morning News,* June 14, 2001)

Bless his heart, he was just trying to explain himself. The poor fellow had a lifeful of losses. He didn't get a fair shake from the dealer; he surely felt at times that the world mistrusted him, doubted him and in the cruelest cut of all, maybe pitied him. He wanted none of that.

So he stuck out his lower lip, stiffened his painful spine and wrote the words:

Out of the night that covers me, Black as the Pit from pole to pole, I thank whatever gods may be For my unconquerable soul.

(Take that, world, and stick it. I don't need your pity. Don't worry about me, babe. Give me your best shot, I can handle it.)

In the fell clutch of circumstance I have not winced nor cried aloud. Under the bludgeonings of chance My head is bloody but unbowed.

As usual, the writer got the most attention for his words years after his lifetime. His words were destined to reach even greater circulation, for all the wrong reasons, just this week.

That stiff upper lip belonged to William Ernest Henley, and he wrote his rhyme before the turn of the last century. He was born in Gloucester in 1849 and the poet Thomas Edward Brown, headmaster at Crypt Grammar School, thought the Henley kid had some promise as a writer.

There were a couple of hitches. The young Henley was stricken with osteomyelitis, a cruel crippling disease that left his body growing out of proportion to his poor withered limbs. At 16, his left leg was amputated below the knee.

• • •

When the lad was 18, his father died and he hobbled to London to get work, to support his mother and five siblings. He found employment as a journalist, but illness struck again and he went to the Royal Edinburgh Infirmary for experimental treatment with antiseptics. Bravely, perhaps defiantly, maybe desperately, he began to write poetry.

Someone brought another young writer to visit Mr. Henley in the hospital, chap named Stevenson. Robert Louis Stevenson. The two writers became great friends. Later they collaborated on four plays. It was believed that Mr. Stevenson, when he wrote his classic *Treasure Island,* patterned Long John Silver on his pal.

Mr. Henley married, had a daughter who died with cerebral meningitis when she was five. Yet another blow to a fellow who had more than his share.

The writer was not a religious man, but he appeared to acknowledge a greater power that controlled the universe. He seemed determined, despite his physical and mental grief, to shrug off the pity of others, to depend upon his own courage to make his way. At least that is the way our schoolboy literature teachers saw it and commanded we commit his lines to memory.

Beyond this place of wrath and tears, looms but the horror of the shade. And yet the menace of the years, finds, and shall find me, unafraid.

• • •

Crippled and sick, Mr. Henley never stopped working, as writer and as editor of several publications. He was a dedicated promoter of a couple of young writers, Rudyard Kipling and Irish poet W. B. Yeats.

Actually, Mr. Henley's most memorable lines, the ones that came into new prominence this week, were a combination of two earlier poems, *A Love by the Sea* and *A Thanksgiving* and were published under the new title *Invictus.*

When Timothy McVeigh went to his just reward this week, amid ghoulish news coverage that would gag a buzzard, he handed the warden a copy of *Invictus.* Those of us who remembered high school English thought Mr. McVeigh's interpretation a gross misconception of Mr. Henley's premise.

Be that as it may, some exalted reporters of the occasion

insinuated the poem was written by Mr. McVeigh himself. At least one accredited it to Robert Frost. "An obscure English poet" was another write-off. Considering this week's interpretation of his words, Mr. Henley probably would have preferred to remain part of that great family of literature called anonymous.

Pressboxers May Resemble That Remark

(*Dallas Morning News,* August 29, 1996)

Perhaps it's not so much the opinion as it is the source of same. Admittedly, the truth wounds. But when it originates from practically a family member, I feel a fraternal obligation to register a protest.

This begins when the venerable sporting author of the *Atlanta Journal-Constitution* takes it upon himself to cast stones upon his caste. When the Olympics departed his city, Furman Bisher bade a mixed bag of adieus. Included in his resume:

"Happily, we've seen the last of old sportswriters walking about in baggy britches and floppy tops," wrote Mr. Bisher. "Sportswriters, worldwide, take the lead in disreputable dress."

Now, it is not the sentiment that prompts a mutter. A relative by marriage once glanced inside a Super Bowl pressroom. "Sloppiest bunch I have ever seen under one roof," said she, wrinkling a delicate nostril.

So it is not that the judgment is being pronounced for the first time, but it was one of our own genre who appointed himself to pound the pulpit.

• • •

Admittedly, the pressbox crowd is rather famous for its, ah, casual attire, ranking above only photographers in the newspaper dodge.

But we have exceptions. The late Doc Greene of Detroit was a fop of wide renown. Doc Greene was the sporting press' answer to Adolphe Menjou, if you remember that dandy. Heavily starched shirts with two-inch cuffs and great heavy links. High shirt collars with a gold cinch pin that seemed to limit cranial circulation, making his eyes bug out like a tromped-on toady frog. High fashion silk suits with pinched waists. Gleaming black wingtips. Cigarette holder. Doc Greene was our fancy pants, and we were proud of him.

166

Arthur Dailey of the *New York Times* was always conventionally garbed. He could have been mistaken for a Supreme Court judge; at least his eyebrows were heavy enough. Damon Runyon, we hear tell, changed his impeccable clothing, from the skin out, three times daily. Red Smith was a neat dresser who would just as soon wear a vest as spit in your eye. Jim Murray, the Left Coast landmark, is never without tie and jacket. Freddie Russell of Nashville, with his delicate gold-rim glasses and manicures, could pass for an art dealer. Lorin McMullen, once of the *Fort Worth Star-Telegram,* was a fashion plate. Dan Jenkins, until he got rich, was right out of Brooks Bros.

However, in all honesty, we mostly are slobs. Typical were two respected authors, Jimmy Cannon of New York and Mo Siegel of Washington. Bless their hearts, both usually wound up looking—as the description often applied to editor Heywood Broun—like an unmade bed.

But for Mr. Bisher to be the one to pronounce judgment may violate some bonds. Example: For four decades, this fellow has worn the same pair of scuffed buckle brogans, made originally for Paul Revere, on the backstretch at Churchill Downs. For years, he arrayed himself in dazzling plaids and loud checks and stripes, *often at the same time.* His robes were colorful as his prose.

I can safely testify that never, never in history has there been a recorded incident of a crow attacking Mr. Bisher in his traditional garb.

Mind you, it wasn't economics that drove Mr. Bisher into his costumes; it was commonly accepted that he would spend as much as $2 for a necktie, providing it was purple. Actually, the gent has propelled himself through the ranks to rare economic status for our grizzled bunch. (He recently endowed his old college with a seven-figure check to further sports journalism, causing near cardiac arrests among his pals.)

So it wasn't finances that drove Mr. Bisher to Jimmy Demaret's garage sales. It was, excuse the expression, taste.

Of course, now that's all changed. A few years ago, the remarkable Linda Bisher joined his household and, obviously,

WRITERS AND FILMMAKERS

has taken the fellow by hand and led him to proper haber-
dasheries. I have it on good authority that Mr. Bisher now is
the proud possessor of a blue blazer and gray slacks and several white shirts and two ties that don't glow in the dark.

Supposedly, this new status entitles him to censor the rest
of us for "disreputable dress," and I, for one, resent it. I don't
deny it, just resent it.

When It Comes to Horror,
Frankenstein Was an Amateur

(*Dallas Morning News,* November 10, 1994)

Here they go again, trying to scare my pants off. Some smart aleck has dug up the poor old Frankenstein monster and is parading him through the countryside once more, maiming various citizens and small livestock, milking us for just one more scream.

Well, it won't work here. In the first place, Frankenstein's creation never did scare the pants off yours very truly. Even back when he was Boris Karloff and towered over everybody and clanked when he walked, I thought him a sympathetic character. I rooted for the poor goof.

Stupid peasants were always poking him with pointed sticks and waving torches in his face. Who could blame him if he occasionally picked up a tormentor and flung him into the next county? All he ever wanted was a hot meal, some fiddle music and a little female companionship. Having served dutifully in the U.S. Navy, I could certainly empathize with that.

Besides, the notices say Robert De Niro is cast as the monster in this current film, and if Mr. De Niro is the fellow I am thinking of, he could walk under your living room coffee table. Mr. Karloff was a tall man for starters, and makeup men added 18 inches to his natural altitude, with stilts and elevator boots and stuff. He was high enough to see over the average cowshed and must have weighed 400 pounds in his stocking feet.

• • •

In the modern motif, the dramatists will probably use scars and twitches and white eyeballs to make the short monster scary, and they will probably throw in an extra bucket of ketchup in hopes we will interpret it as gore. No sale here.

There must have been 109 sequels in the threescore years

since the original production. (Would you believe *Abbott and Costello Meet Frankenstein?*) There was even a hilarious comedy by Mel Brooks that cast the monster as a song-and-dance man. But nothing approached the classic first version.

Besides, the composition of the *Frankenstein* novel always appealed to us romanticists. The way we heard it, a winsome British teen-ager named Mary Wollstonecraft ran off to Switzerland with a married chap called Percy Bysshe Shelley, whom you remember from your sixth-grade English class. This was in the early 1800s, before public hanky-panky became popular.

Anyway, they were shacked up in a lake house owned by Lord Byron when the three of them were marooned by a weekend of horrible weather. They were lounging around looking bored, probably drinking and smoking too much, when Lord Byron suggested each write a ghost story as a sort of indoor weekend project.

*Frankens*tein was Ms. Wollstonecraft's contribution, although it wasn't published until a few years later, when she and ole Percy were legally hitched.

• • •

Actually, the real, honest-to-goodness reason that Frankenstein couldn't scare my pants off is that they had already been dropped by Count Dracula. Now *there* was a genuine terror.

Never mind these modern spooks with scissors hands or that silly Freddie Krueger rising up from the lake with moss on his face. Bela Lugosi was the *real thing* as Count Dracula, with his slicked-back hair and his black brows and piercing eyes and his evil accent.

For weeks, I would wake up and see those eyes staring from the foot of the bed. People may talk about delicious horror, but there wasn't anything *delicious* about Mr. Lugosi. He would cause you to review your past sins and pray feverishly for daylight.

There was another, practical reason to a child exposed to

these two threats. In juvenile logic, it would be fairly easy to outrun the clumsy Frankenstein monster, stumbling around with his arms stuck out and his eyes at half-mast. But how could you flee from Count Dracula, who could change into a wolf or a bat anytime he dang well pleased?

It was pitch dark when I got out of the picture show after seeing *Dracula,* and not a soul was on the street. The family tepee was exactly one mile from the movie. They claim I was clocked at 4:04, which wasn't at all bad, considering I was in swaddling clothes, slick shoes and running up a slight incline. I distinctly remember passing a couple of low-flying bats along the way.

Star Trek

(Dallas Times Herald, June 4, 1984)

Well, here it is exactly one week later and the telephone hasn't rung. Surely there has been a breakdown in communications.

It was Tuesday last that several of us, shall we say, *seasoned* pressboxers became Movie Stars or very near. From various pressboxes about the land we were summoned to Atlanta to star in a baseball movie called *The Slugger's Wife.*

Maybe *star* isn't the correct verb. Actually, we were typecast. We were assigned roles of sportswriters following the exploits of an Atlanta Brave slugger, Darryl Palmer, played by a rather plain chap named Michael O'Keefe, as he was closing in on Roger Maris' home run record. As near as we could tell, this was the primary background of the drama, although it also dealt with rock-and-roll singers and occasional rolls in the old hay.

However, the writer Neil Simon must be aware of the strict moral code endorsed by The Froth Estate, so he did not include us in the romantic scenes. This came as a marked disappointment to some of our more daring members, such as Furman Bisher, the distinguished Atlanta author and part-time *amoureaux* who has been known to carry a hand mirror in his pants pocket.

Anyways, even if we were withheld from the heavy breathing, we felt assured we would be accorded large, important roles. It was the general hunch that we would be used in a big dramatic scene, like maybe a press interview after a record homer with hero Palmer or maybe the Atlanta manager Burly de Vito, played by a placid veteran named Martin Ritt, who put his hands in his back uniform pockets just like real-life managers.

Surely we would have speaking roles. Mr. Bob Verdi, a rather foxy thespian from the *Chicago Tribune,* thought he should be the reporter at the press conference to stand and deliver our favorite question of such events:

"What was going through your mind when you were circling the bases?"

Privately I had written my own opening soliloquy: "What happened?" It's really not the number of words you have, but how you say them.

Both interior and exterior scenes were being filmed at the Braves Stadium and we were on the set by eight ayem, ready for makeup. Instead, we were shunted aside while a small army of technicians milled. As any of us movie folk can tell you, there is a large amount of milling done, at union scale. One chap kept peddling a bicycle by our group, yelling over his shoulder, "Check with Caleb!" For two hours this was the most interesting conversation we heard.

Finally, some pleasant assistant broke the news. There would be no speaking lines. Instead, he stationed small groups of us by the dugout, and by the coaching box, and by the bat rack and on-deck circle and explained that this would be a scene in which hero Darryl Palmer gets beaned in batting practice. In batting practice?

Anyways, all clusters of pressboxers would be chatting with this ballplayer, or that, and when the star got beaned, we were to rush to the batting cage.

"Look aghast, please!" said a young fellow with a bullhorn. "Be perfectly natural and do not look into the camera or into the sun." This may sound easy to *you*.

Your budding thespian here was stationed with Mr. John Mooney, a 300-pound ham from the *Salt Lake City Tribune* and Mr. Hal Block of the AP and Mr. Jim Smith of *Newsday* at one corner of the dugout. A friendly lad in a Braves uniform was assigned as our interview target. He turned out to be one Andre Pattillo, who spent a couple seasons in the Atlanta farm system and is now employed as a counselor with the Educational Opportunity Center.

Bisher and Verdi managed a spot much nearer the camera, of course, but still were outmaneuvered by Phil Pepe and Murray Chass, who are from New York and experienced in pushing. Bob Roesler of New Orleans and Dick Fenlon of

Columbus were assigned strolling roles, which promptly went to their heads.

Of course we had 413 walk-throughs and long waits in between during which Mooney practiced looking aghast until he had it down pat. He also shot a critical eye at the situation and estimated our group was 732 feet from the camera with Pepe and Chass edging in front and blotting out the lens.

Then there came the action! The batting practice pitcher faked a throw, Mr. Michael O'Keefe winced and fell poleaxed (on a couple air mattresses the prop man had placed in the cage). We all rushed to the batting cage. Verdi and Bisher practically sprinted, figuring early arrivals would be prominent on camera.

From the rear of the crowd, I remembered my soliloquy and offered it as an added attraction. After all, I could be spotted by some bigshot director and made into another Cary Grant or Lash LaRue.

"What happened?" I said, not unlike Charles Bronson.

"Stuck it in his *bleeping* ear!" growled Mike Downey, a coarse chap from the *Detroit Free Press*. Method actor.

Apparently the cameras and microphones did not capture this impromptu act because no one has called with any sort of career proposition. Dear Diary: What's to become of me?

This and That

Perspectives from an Armchair Sociologist

Sometimes, Discretion Seems More Important than Valor

(Dallas Morning News, October 20, 1994)

Had a vote been taken, the prettiest lady in town would have been Hattie Belle Pinkston. She had short red hair, always precisely set in waves. Her complexion, rare in those mean, scorched parts, was peach ice cream. She wore neat silk dresses and almost never said a word except "thank you."

Her family name, before she married Slim Pinkston, was Smith. And her brother Donk was fullback on the high school team—and, in later years, a career Marine. (Once I chanced upon Donk at a distant place called Guadalcanal, where he exercised his authority as mess sergeant to have his cook grill me a beefsteak fit for a prince—or maybe even a lieutenant commander. But that's another story.)

Hattie Belle Pinkston was the cashier in our little town's only movie, and she sat demurely in her glass cage and accepted your dime and slid your ticket through the opening with graceful hands, just a hint of freckles under her nice Bulova wristwatch.

Most thought hers was a plush job in hard times because there was a soft stool in the cage and an electric fan and because, after the last feature started, she could close her booth, go inside and watch the movie, while she waited for her husband.

Slim was the movie's projectionist, a tall, spare, sandy fellow isolated in a lonely cell at the back of the balcony, changing reels and patching film. Like his missus, Slim talked very little.

After Hoot Gibson whupped the last rustler, Slim and Hattie Belle would lock up and walk three blocks to the town's only midnight oasis.

• • •

THIS AND THAT

Crows Café stayed open all night because it was also the Greyhound bus stop. The place had few late customers, for ours were hard-working folk who believed in a good night's sleep except for Saturdays, when there was a fair amount of hoops and hollers.

The normal midnight would find Hattie Belle and Slim drinking coffee in silence, and maybe she would have a slice of lemon meringue pie, and Slim would smoke his Camel cigarettes. It was generally agreed that Slim was about as good a Camel smoker as there was around.

Usually there would be another fellow called Ugg, for obvious reasons, who drove the town's only taxi. And there was Crow, a chunky, bald cynic who was apt to buy you a bottle of Pearl if he liked you—or poke you on the nose if he didn't.

Crows Café was one big room, and in the back corners, one on each side, were stairways leading up to the restrooms.

One midnight, Crow was hunched over the counter, chewing a toothpick and reading a newspaper, Ugg was nodding, Hattie Belle was eating her pie and Slim was smoking his Camels when the door burst open and a fat, florid fellow in suit and tie demanded a Pearl beer at the top of his voice.

Through the plate-glass window, in the drive circle, they could see a long, black Packard with a chauffeur in the driver's seat. Crow looked at the customer briefly and shook his head.

"Ah'm the owner of King Ranch!" shouted the fellow, "and ah want a Pearl beer!" Crow sighed and said no dice, friend, and "I don't care if you own the Panama Canal, it's after 12 o'clock."

"Ah'll get my shotgun and kill every clodhopper in this place!" said the man, staggering to the door. Hattie Belle and Slim and Crow traded glances, perhaps grateful for this little break in their tedium. Crow hunched back over his paper, and suddenly the door flew back, and here was the man waving the biggest shotgun on earth.

• • •

Well, sir, activity began, you might say. Hattie Belle dropped to the floor and crawled under her table. Ugg beat it through the swinging kitchen doors, and Crow ducked behind the counter. Slim stood up in some confusion, then dashed for the back of the room and ran up the stairs.

Once there, to his great horror, Slim discovered that he was in the ladies' room. With cheeks the color of a Christmas stocking, he stumbled back down the stairs, ran all the way across the room in front of the threatening shotgun and up the left-hand stairs to the men's room where he belonged.

For years, the story was retold by the citizenry, and not altogether out of ridicule. There also was a slight respect for Mr. Pinkston, who was more proper than prudent, but in times and towns that were the same.

The Good Doctor

(*Dallas Morning News,* May 16, 1996)

With each passing year, the urge to blow one's top becomes fainter. Firstly, it requires much energy, of which there seems a shorter supply. Secondly, there are so many blown tops in this dodge, there is always the probability that the explosion will go unnoticed.

However, I still can muster sufficient indignation when I hear some jock millionaire proclaim, "Why, if it wasn't for football, I could not have gotten a college education. I'd be out on the street."

When I hear this attempt to be humble, I have this overpowering urge to shout above the crowd as follows: "What a crock!"

The physical ability to catch a leather ball or crush a nearby sternum, thereby gaining athletic free rides, makes it *easier* to acquire a $100,000 diploma. But it is not, by any means, the *only* way for a strong but poor chap (who can read without moving his lips) to get a higher education. Or even an undersized, weak youngster. The education is there for the taking, if the resolve is strong enough. Key word: If.

This thought resurfaced last weekend when I returned to a Central Texas campus to monitor 244 youngsters receiving college diplomas. It had been a couple of centuries since I attended those rites, but you could sense a sameness of concern among these lads and lassies, i.e., leaving the college cocoon and finding work in a dwindling job market. As it so happened with us, World War II happened along about that time and kindly solved the employment problem for the next few years.

• • •

Usually, when one revisits a scene of youth, he finds that surroundings have shrunk. Buildings are smaller, rivers narrower, streets far less imposing. But in the case of Howard

Payne University in Brownwood, the opposite prevails. The campus has swollen. Where there were three classroom buildings, an auditorium for daily (and compulsive) chapel services, a gym, a women's dormitory and some ramshackle wooden buildings, now there is a compact, bustling little city. It still is not a wealthy place, but somehow Dr. Don Newbury and his crew find ways to make the considerable ends meet.

The old Howard Payne College was not Hahvud. It was not Texas A&M. But it was, and remains, a kindly, immensely helpful place to further one's book learning. And it was the epitome of my personal premise: If you can pass tests, you can get a college degree.

It may not be at the institution of first choice; it may not be in the allotted four years. Heck, you might have to drop out a year or so to work and save money. You might have to work part-time jobs and take some night courses. But if you want the sheepskin desperately and can make passing grades, you can find a place that will accommodate you.

Howard Payne was such a place in those old days. There was a fellow named Cap Shelton who held the fort together. He was everything—business manager, professor, hustler, track coach, whatever. If you wanted an education and were willing to work, Cap would see that you got it. There were no student loans at the time, but there were dishes to be washed, maintenance to be done, stores to be clerked. Cap would somehow find a job for you. A lot of us owe him. And I'd be surprised if Don Newbury and his bunch are not in the same mode today.

• • •

Earlier this year, Dr. Newbury somehow decided it was about time this old goat changed billing, thereby proving his remarkable sense of humor. Since it was at Howard Payne that an assistant coach named Clarence McCarver slapped my dratted nickname on me, Dr. Newbury thought it only fair that his be the place to change same. He suggested doctor of something or other with a robe and mantle and the works. Doctor of

THIS AND THAT

Letters, I think. It came as a vague disappointment to a few old pals who showed up that I would be unable to write prescriptions.

Somewhere in the blue, we can be sure that Cap Shelton and Eula Haskew and Cleo McCristy and McAdoo Keaton and Gladys Hicks and Dr. Havins all gathered together and said to Dr. Newbury, in unison: "You did what?????"

At any rate, the old nickname may be discarded. A simple "doctor" will now suffice. The perfunctory tug of forelock is optional.

Real Pros Pick More than Winners

(*Dallas Morning News,* January 23, 1997)

The late Jack Hurley was a delightful scoundrel. As a fight manager, he was quick to appreciate larceny in his fellow men.

Mr. Hurley lived in a Seattle hotel room, hatching such stings as promoting an amateur, Pete Rademacher, into a match for the world heavyweight title. This scam aroused quiet pride in Mr. Hurley, who ranked it up there with Teapot Dome and Clifford Irving.

Our man was on a Seattle street one fine day, when he was gently bumped. A block later, he stopped, flew his hands over his body, turned and took off in a high lope. Whatever he was pursuing, he didn't catch.

"Imagine me, Jack Hurley, getting my pocket picked!" he cried. "It's against nature! He had to go through my overcoat, under my suit and into my pants. It's indecent!"

"Well," said a guy, "even if you caught him, you couldn't get him arrested. He woulda ditched the wallet."

"Hell, this guy is a champion!" yelled Mr. Hurley. "I don't want to arrest him, I want to manage him!"

• • •

The story returns because of this particular week. The nation's sporting press will descend on Noo Awleans for Super Box XXXI, which means the local pickpockets, and many imported ones, are drooling like groupies at an autograph show. For some weird reason, pressboxers are considered prime targets by the lightfingers.

We have given this puzzle considerable thought. Surely, it is not because we look or act prosperous, not even on an expense account. Neither is it occupational naiveté, because we spend most working hours among cheats of some sort, whether a pitcher scarring a baseball or a franchise owner selling personal seat licenses. The only logical conclusion is that the pickpockets use us as warm-up exercises, as a hitter takes batting practice.

Most of us have been victims. I was knocked off in this same Noo Awleens during a Final Four tournament. Old trick. I was boarding a hotel elevator when a young chap suddenly decided to disembark, and we moved back and forth, trying to get out of the other's path. While I was intent on maneuvering, a compadre behind me entered my left front pocket and removed a money clip. More than outrage, I was filled with admiration and a certain amount of shame, especially later when the interrogating officer inspected my hair for corn shucks.

The same trick was pulled on Edwin Pope of Miami, this at a Final Four tournament in Denver. He was trying to disembark the elevator, and a youth pulled the confused dance. Mr. Pope felt a nudge, grabbed at his hip and bellowed like a gored ox. He clapped his hand on the elevator control and declaimed to fellow occupants: "Somebody on this elevator just picked my pocket! If I don't get my wallet back by the time I count ten, I am pressing the emergency button, and we all go to the cops!"

When he reached "five," he heard a slight thump, and one lad said, "Why, here it is on the floor. It must have fallen out of your pocket." Of course, the thief had dumped it.

Once at a Super Bowl, Paul Zimmerman of *Sports Illustrated* had his pocket cleaned, and this caused much concern because he was holding the contributions from the press-room game pool. Jimmy Cannon was hit at a Madison Square Garden card. Dan Cook of San Antonio was working ringside at the Hagler-Hearn fight when he was picked. Randy Galloway, representing this paper at a New York World Series, got it in his hotel's revolving door, for goodness sakes. There have been countless others.

Of course, some of us are trained to be wary. Jim Murray, the Left Coast poet, had covered the Indy 500. At the airline counter, the clerk was preparing his ticket when he was aware of a nudge on his right hip. Quickly, Mr. Murray felt his empty pocket and wheeled to the man behind him.

"I got you! Gimme back my wallet!" he yelled. "Give it back right now, or I'm calling a cop!"

The fellow looked at him in astonishment, and then the writer heard the soft voice of the airline lady over his shoulder.

"Excuse me, sir, is this what you're looking for?" She was holding the wallet that Mr. Murray had placed on the counter to remove his credit card. Mr. Murray blushed so hard, he later peeled.

Has This Really Become the Best of All Possible Worlds?

(*Dallas Morning News*, February 6, 1997)

It is difficult to measure the scope of our relief to learn that civilization finally has righted itself. The sun is back in its heaven, after being AWOL for a considerable spell, and this suddenly is the best of all possible worlds.

Incidentally, the Chinese say this is the Year of the Ox, but we beg the populace to ignore this. Last time we had the Year of the Ox, Shiites and Palestinians were hijacking planes and ships all over the place, mudslides were burying Colombia, and Sylvester Stallone failed to get an Oscar for *Rambo*. We certainly do not want to go through *that* again.

We shade-tree philosophers sensed the return of Camelot when, according to the testimony of several young men in green clothes, the Almighty made it possible for them to take the sainted Lombardi Trophy to Wisconsin. Right then, we suspected the world was in tiptop shape if the Almighty could leave his workplace and concern himself with a football match.

• • •

Further proof that national problems are kaput is the fact that the Rev. Jesse Jackson gave considerable study to the Dennis Rodman case. News hounds, fresh out of Mideast bombings, recently concentrated on Mr. Rodman putting the boot to a fellow man. Mr. Rodman is a Chicago basketball player with green hair, a ring in his nose and occasional false eyelashes. During a recent game, he felt it necessary to kick a photographer in his vital zone. For this foul deed, he was fined a fortune and expelled for 11 games.

Now the world is purring so smoothly, Rev. Jackson could take time off from settling Texaco problems and advising Yasser Arafat to issue counsel on the Rodman case. "Let Rodman play," he said, presumably speaking to NBA president

David Stern. "It's one thing to punish a man and another thing to take away his dignity."

This one statement establishes Rev. Jackson as one of the outstanding comedians of our time and leads us to presume the Chinese to have made a typographical error. This actually must be the Year of the Oxymoron.

• • •

Then after futilely combing the news for further world worries, we settle for a former well-scrubbed soda jerk becoming a reborn coonshouter. Last time we saw Pat Boone, he was an angel in *The Greatest Story Ever Told*. Before that, he was constantly before us in his white bucks, eating apple pie, drinking milk and singing *Love Letters in the Sand*. He got his hair cut every day, saw his dentist twice a week and went to prayer meeting on Wednesday.

Now after 30 years of relative obscurity, Mr. Boone appears shirtless in ponytail and tattoo and singing something called "heavy metal." My only concept of rock music is a bunch of half-naked Piltdown chaps leaping around a smoky stage, perspiring freely, busting gittars over neighbors' skulls and eating live frogs.

Obviously, there is more to it. The *Dictionary of American Pop/Rock* says that a fellow named Jimi Hendrix is the granddaddy of heavy metal and that his crowning moment came in one concert when he burned out four amplifiers. There was more, but I found that to be a reasonable stopping place.

At any rate, Mr. Boone announced he has made the switch to sweat and found himself on the front pages and leading the newscasts. My private financial analyst estimates that Mr. Boone received approximately $8,835,003 in free advertising within two days, assuring the sale of 10,533,00 heavy metal albums.

Now you are beginning to see the light. Perhaps the last 30 years have not been lucrative for Mr. Boone. Maybe *Love Letters* doesn't pay the rent anymore. So this harks back to an oft-repeated bit of philosophy in my notebook:

187

Sammy Renick, a seasoned jockey in Florida, was listening to a fellow rider celebrating his final appearance. Said he: "I've saved my money. I'll never get up at four in the morning, I'll never diet again, I'll never take another steam bath, I'll never get up on another horse."

"Don't ever say never," advised wise old Sammy Renick. "Hard times will make a monkey eat red pepper."

Geezer Generation Gets Biggest Slice of the Experience Cake

(Dallas Morning News, February 13, 1997)

If you've been staying awake nights, trying to classify your generation, fret no longer. I have done it for you and herewith advise you to be amazed at your times. Count not just your blessings but your adventures. Your headlines.

We still have the Geezers roaming their pastures, plus Baby Boomers and Protesters and the *Ubi Est Mea* (where's mine?) generation and Soccer Moms and Driveby Shooters and the White House Overnighters. But it is Geezers who occupy the throne of which we marvel.

After lengthy research and considerable mulling, I am prepared to announce that the Geezers, and maybe the early Baby Boomers, have been history's most experienced generation.

This is not to say all events have been good and wholesome and advantageous to civilization. To borrow from Mr. Charles Dickens: It has been the best of times and the worst of times. But the times are unmatched in the *number* of extraordinary happenings.

A generation encompasses about 30 years. That being the yardstick, the Geezers may consider themselves as history's most eventful bracket. That is, if your age is around three-score, you have experienced more newsworthy events than any other class. No generation has witnessed so many startling events, such headlines, such revolutionary developments, in one lifetime. Think about it.

• • •

Of course we had wars. All generations have a war or two. But *we* had a war *with an atomic bomb,* surely the most devastating weapon of all time. We had the jet engine and jet missiles, which, in a single jolt, eliminated this nation's two bulwarks of defense—the Atlantic and the Pacific.

189

We had the unbelievable progress of the automobile. We experienced the birth of talking pictures and, more astounding, the advent of television. Think of what TV has done to our daily lives. I can remember a casual conversation under a Pacific palm in the mid-'40s when a freshly minted radar officer speculated that someday moving pictures would be bounced off the atmosphere right into our living rooms. Yeah, sure, we said.

The powdered wigs had their headlines, but they couldn't match us in numbers and dimension. You can imagine, perhaps, a conversation between Benjamin Franklin and Thomas Jefferson in a Philadelphia pub. Mr. Franklin suggests to Mr. Jefferson that someday a human would walk on the moon. You can just see Mr. Jefferson picking up his pint and moving to the other side of the room, from where he stares at Mr. Franklin with what is popularly known in banking circles as a fishy eye. Yet our generation hit golf balls on the moon.

We had a president quit his office in disgrace and another one slain. No other generation has witnessed so many assassinations and assassination attempts of national leaders here and abroad.

We gave birth to air conditioning! Wonderful, blessed air conditioning. We first experienced integration. The Internet, whatever that is. Computers. Fax. Synthetics. Penicillin. Frozen foods. Terrorist bombings. Contact lenses. Steroids. Crack. AIDS. Income tax.

Perhaps just three or four of these rascals might occur to one generation, but the whole batch? I think not.

• • •

These generations now in session, those born in the '60s, '70s and '80s, could possibly top us. It may become normal for folks to live to be 100, and physician-assisted suicides may be legal and commonplace.

The current class will possibly experience a cancer cure and a gasoline substitute. It may live to see the end of an Anglo-run Earth and the start of Asian domination. California may slide into the sea, and several states may make a serious move to secede from the union. The currents could probably win the title if asteroids crashed somewhere in Siberia, if a weather balloon lands in Pennsylvania and little green men pop forth.

It is not out of the question that a younger batch may replace us as the most adventurous generation. But it will take considerable doing.

Mind Reading Should Go to the Dogs

(*Dallas Morning News,* March 6, 1997)

One remembered proof of the pudding came in a midnight seminar on an ancient Cowboy road trip. You might be surprised at some topics earning our expert consideration. On this night, the subject was presidential possibilities, and Tex Schramm mentioned Henry Kissinger. From some chair came a hasty disclaimer that Mr. Kissinger wasn't eligible because he was foreign-born.

Mr. Schramm turned to a newcomer on the fringe of the group. "Is that right?" he asked. "Does that disqualify him?"

"Hey, why would you ask him?" said a miffed panelist. "Why wouldn't you think one of *us* would know?"

Tex gave it some thought. "Well," he said lamely, "he has a beard."

The Cowboy president had bought the popular theory of those days that anyone who grew a beard was automatically an intellectual. Furthermore, the fellow wore a tie. A beard and a tie in tandem were undeniable marks of superior brainpower. And if he happened also to smoke a pipe, forget it. He's not one of us.

Therefore, I paid respectful heed the other night when a fellow in a beard and tie (and, I suspect, a pipe in his pocket) came on the boob toob to forecast weird futures for personal computers. Someday soon, he said, you may sit in front of your screen and ask it a question. Not punch it on the keyboard but *ask* it. The computer will read your voice and flash the answer.

• • •

Not only that, said the fellow in the beard and tie and pipe in pocket, some years later, you will be able to confront your computer and *think* of a problem. The computer will *read your mind* and give the answer. I did not dream this up.

Now, this would be one case where I strongly endorse animal laboratory testing. I propose that this mind-reading computer first be tested on dogs, and I hasten to volunteer the two who live at our house. Being a devoted researcher in these matters, I would give anything, save the remote channel flicker and my complete collection of James Thurber books, to learn what a dog is thinking.

All dog folk are similarly afflicted. The world has no mystery to match dog eyes. Every master has stared in those dark caves and wondered what it going on behind them. Is he thinking: (a) *Oh, how I love this big lug because he takes good care of me,* or (b) *This bum got a lotta nerve, feeding me dry pellets that would gag a hyena while he chews on a thick sirloin?*

For example, there is one prominent school of thought that a dog is devoted to whomever feeds him. I would amend that theory to whomever feeds him and scratches him behind the ears. But occasionally you wonder if the attachment goes deeper.

• • •

All dog people have stories that bore you to tears. Back when I traveled frequently, I was under constant surveillance during the packing chore. I would place the bag on the bed. The family dog, a poodle at the time, would lie on the pillows, head on paws, motionless except for eyes, following every move. To the bureau and back to the bag, to the closet and back, to the bathroom and back.

When I arrived at whatever destination, heaved the bag on the hotel bed and started to unpack, there would be, burrowed among the underwear and socks, some sort of dog toy. A rag doll perhaps, a favorite tennis ball or a leather chewing thong.

While my back was turned, the poodle would sneak a treasure in the bag. Whether she was hoping to go along on the trip or whether she simply wanted to send a reminder that she was back home and probably hungry. Whatever her motive, it was enough to make your throat ache.

With this new computer function, we would be privy to the

THIS AND THAT

secrets. The guys with the beard and tie and pipe could tell us, when the spaniel stands at the back door and watches you unlock the car, is she worrying that you never will return? Or is she saying, goody, the big lummox is leaving and now I can dig that steak bone out of the garbage and take a nap on the forbidden couch? All things considered, perhaps it's best we do not know.

If You Believe Everything You See, Do I Have a Deal for You

(*Dallas Morning News,* October 16, 1997)

The text of today's sermon, you were taught at your father's knee. Especially if your father was Chinese.

"One picture is worth more than ten thousand words," sayeth the wise old man, quoting Confucius or Cecil DeMille.

Well, it cometh to pass that your old man, in today's marketplace, would go broke buying pigs in pokes. These days, if you believe pictures, you are a ripe prospect to corner the beach cabana market in North Dakota. The word market may be making a comeback.

Personally, mine eyes have seen Fred Astaire dancing with a vacuum cleaner, although researchers claim he came no nearer to such than the appliance pages in the Sears Roebuck catalog.

However, there is no doubt about it being Mr. Astaire, take it from old dad here. I once rode up in an elevator with him in the Knickerbocker Hotel at Ivor and Vine in Hollywood, Calif. This was Fred all righty, there on the telly, natty in his black-and-white shoes and straw hat, dancing up a storm while caressing this dust buster like it was Ginger Rogers.

I also have personally seen actual film of John Wayne stalking into a saloon and cadging a lite beer off a bully, while Ben Cartwright and his tribe backed him up. And just last week, we all saw the TV commercial with none other than Ed Sullivan introducing, on stage, a 1997 luxury car. Some of us chillun thought Mr. Sullivan had been rather dead for years, but there he was—plain as day. There is another old saying: Pictures don't lie.

* * *

Not long ago, we watched actual film of this Forrest Gump fellow visiting the White House and asking President John F.

Kennedy if he could use the royal loo. The president, sensing his guest was a Democrat, laughed and pointed down the hall.

Just as us bewildered masses mill in confusion, believing our eyes as we were taught, comes word that this hoax is a product of something called "digital technology," wherein video images are manipulated to a frightening degree. It's another of those wicked things that computers are taught to do. This supports our theory that computers were sent to Earth by another planet, with the avowed intent of driving us bonkers so the aliens can land and send us all to work camp.

For years, we have been aware of what retouch artists can do with an airbrush on a photo. "Image enhancement," they call it. For years, they could take four inches off the hips of Ingrid Bergman or, if hucksters demanded it for lobby posters, completely remove the head of Claudette Colbert and fit it atop the body of Miss America, 1963.

Also, it doesn't rupture the imagination to see the coloring altered in movies. You may remember Ted Turner buying such black-and-white classics as *Casablanca* and hiring artists to retouch the film in color.

During his murder trial, the mug of O.J. Simpson appeared on the cover of a news magazine, and Simpson supporters screamed that retouch artists had darkened his skin color to emphasize his race. On the other hand, just recently Whoopi Goldberg raised ole billy because a magazine artist had lightened her skin in a cover photo. I tell you, it is not a peaceful world.

The digital technicians are not stealing dimes off dead eyes. The managers of Mr. Astaire's and Mr. Wayne's estates and such are paid for the rights and have approval of the process. One of the Wayne boys takes the editing seriously, manipulating the computer this way and that. But the possibilities seem a bit frightening. If computers can take the walking cane out of Mr. Astaire's hand and substitute a vacuum cleaner, then in the next presidential campaign, some political commercial may show a candidate in bed with a camel.

Wise men once advised that we not believe anything we

hear or read and only half of what we see. But now, you can't even buy that half. What's to believe, anymore?

Which may be what the Chinese meant by another maxim: He who travels by land is eaten by tiger. He who travels by water is eaten by crocodile.

Some Ties Bind Society Too Tightly

(Dallas Morning News, January 28, 1999)

Ever so cautiously, like a prairie dog emerging after a stampede, our cell members are admitting their persuasion.

For years, we met in mean basements, using secret handshakes and code names. To paraphrase Kermit the Frog: it wasn't easy being a disciple of the Tie Liberation Army.

Years ago, this gallant group was formed right here, right in this very corner. A half-dozen stalwarts took a grim oath against wearing the cursed neckties in our daily pursuits. Free the Adam's apple to roam free as the breeze, maybe freer. Be able to look full port or starboard without moving our shoulders and without our eyes bugging out like a tromped-on toad frog.

Our patron saints were Ted Williams and Bill Veeck, two baseball gents who refused to wear ties, regardless of the occasion. Candles flickered below their portraits.

From the start, we were shouted down, derided by conformists, haberdashers and some womenfolk. Countess Mara burned crosses on our lawns. There was talk of branding an S on our foreheads. S for slob.

The TLA made an attempt to compromise, voting to exempt funerals and formal dinners. Still, we were scorned.

• • •

Then, gradually, we could see cracks in the proud ramparts. Dallas businesses were known internationally for insisting on "proper" attire for their employees. Shoe clerks dressed like Wall Street brokers. Downtown, at five o'clock, an army of clones in dark suits, starched white shirts and striped ties spilled from corporate caves onto the streets, like a scene from a Japanese science-fiction movie.

But even in this hostile area, certain signs were noted. Companies began Dress Down Fridays, wherein employees were allowed to dress casually one day a week. For males, the necktie was the first to go.

The Dallas Salesmanship Club is accepted as the city's foremost collection of power brokers. Yet, at one recent summer meeting, TLA mole Joe Worsham counted 34 unbound necks. When Sgt. Worsham reported this breakthrough to TLA troops, he was roundly applauded, and dry eyes were scarce.

Last summer, at a Fort Worth City Council session, Mayor Kenneth Barr, may his tribe increase, tore the yoke from his throat and passionately declared a moratorium on neckties until Labor Day.

Then, by gollies, we invaded royalty.

• • •

Perhaps you noted how Prince Claus of the Netherlands, speaking at a fashion show last month, ripped the navy blue necktie from his neck and flung it at the feet of his spouse, Queen Beatrix. This was no impulsive move by a rebellious youth. The prince is 73 and obviously had given the matter long consideration.

"A snake around my neck!" he shouted. He got a standing ovation. Reporting the incident later, a television anchorman tore off his own tie, and so did the sportscaster in the midst of his soccer scores.

"Claustrophilia" is the name for the prince's denouncement, and it is spreading throughout his land. Delft businessman Wouter van Winden joined the move with, "I'm shouting for joy at the prince's call for a ban on neckties. No piece of clothing performs so little function. For me, a necktie is like a dog leash that symbolizes a limit on freedom."

"Why else," he cried, "does Nelson Mandela never wear one?" An inspired reference, to be sure.

TLA monitors were delighted at the NFC championship game. Normally, the big shots dress to the hilt for this auspicious affair. Yet when TV cameras found Red McCombs in his luxurious box, the Minnesota owner was coatless and tieless and his shirt unbuttoned to a comfortable degree. At the

THIS AND THAT

biggest moment of his business life, he was a man in a rocking chair on his back porch.

As the game turned out, it was rather fortunate that Mr. McCombs was not wearing a tie or he might have hanged himself. As the Tie Liberation Army is proud to stress, there is no end to its benefits.

Signs of the Times

(*Dallas Morning News,* May 27, 1999)

At the calculated risk of political incorrectness, let us say hooray for our side.

When one takes a stand these days, one is wary of snipers behind every bush. It doesn't take much for "students" to mount a protest in front of your gate. Incidentally, this brings up an old curiosity: These "students," who seem to abound in every city in every land, when do they ever go to class? What do they study? Spray painting? Rock tossing? Whisker growing? The science of existing without bath water?

Chancing all that censure, it still is Our Side's duty to applaud certain spectators at a recent National Hockey League playoff. Normally, one doesn't find much drollery in hockey crowds; they are more given to ill-tempered growls and thrown objects. But here were some Colorado partisans holding a large sign: "WHETHER YOU WIN OR LOSE, YOU STILL HAVE TO LIVE IN DETROIT."

Now *that's* funny. No doubt the sentiment brought protests from Red Wing rooters, but it's still funny to compare living in the unbridled beauty of Colorado with existence in Detroit or, in truth, almost anywhere else.

• • •

It brought to mind another memorable sign, this at a Texas-SMU football contest. This one was in response to sneers that SMU students were snobs, given to wealthy backgrounds, chinos, alligator knits and burnished loafers and not much football talent. While squads warmed up on the floor of ritzy Texas Stadium, a big placard was raised in the Mustang cheering section: "OUR MAID WENT TO TEXAS." That one entered the scrapbook.

Another prize goes to the 24-Hour Fitness folk in San Francisco who decorated a big billboard with the simple message: "WHEN THEY COME, THEY'LL EAT THE FAT ONES FIRST." Of course, this caused a protest from Bay Area folk, some with expanded waistlines and others eager to protest even before they learn the reason thereof.

• • •

And then there are the "God" signboards originated by a Fort Lauderdale advertising agency and financed by a client who somehow has managed to remain anonymous. Motorists were exposed to such messages as:

"LET'S MEET AT MY HOUSE SUNDAY BEFORE THE GAME—GOD."

"YOU THINK IT'S HOT HERE?—GOD."

"KEEP USING MY NAME IN VAIN, I'LL MAKE RUSH HOUR LONGER—GOD."

Oh, there were mild protesters as usual. But many of us, perhaps *most* of us, said, hey, lighten up, a little laughter is balm for the soul.

The God Speaking idea became so popular that the Dallas Outdoor Advertising Association donated 100 billboards to carry the messages through the spring months:

"LOVED THE WEDDING, INVITE ME TO THE MAR-RIAGE—GOD."

"HAVE YOU READ MY NUMBER 1 BESTSELLER? THERE WILL BE A TEST—GOD."

"NEED DIRECTIONS?—GOD."

Of course, as with any successful program, there were imitators tainting the idea with commercialism. An animal rights group in Amarillo prepared a board: "JESUS WAS A VEGETAR-IAN." The message lasted three days before the signboard folks bowed to the considerable meat industry. There were threats to retaliate with a picture of children saying grace over a big T-bone: "THANK YOU LORD FOR THE BEEF ON OUR TABLE."

Perhaps you noticed, in one photo from the Oklahoma tornado devastation, there was a deviation of one message. On the surviving wall of a battered building, someone had scrawled in big black lettering: "GOD, WE NEED TO TALK."

BLACKIE SHERROD AT LARGE

Probably that stunt, in the face of such disaster, brought protests from some. Others of us applaud. In humor there is strength.

In fact, as soon as I win the lottery, I will buy a billboard of my own and use my scrapbook's most inspirational message:

It's easy to grin, when your ship comes in. Or you have the stock market beat. But the man worthwhile is the man who can smile, when his shorts are too tight in the seat. Amen.

Marketing Wizards Stay a Step Ahead

(*Dallas Morning News,* January 2, 1997)

In the throes of national politics and our role as world referee and the O.J. Simpson series, it may have escaped your attention that we are under a merchandising siege. These developments creep up on you like flour-sack drawers until suddenly you are their captive.

While we were being flogged by the surgeon general, while we retreat pale and trembling from the evil clutch of cigarettes, when we finally quit the dratted things and breathe relief, we look over and see Mr. Cigar in the next bed. Come into my parlor, says he, smiling benignly.

Oh, this is not to say the cigar folk are claiming immunity to cancer. Nothing so extreme. It's my inexpert guess that *some* body, some brilliant merchandiser, saw all those zillion cigarette quitters as terrific market potential and set out to woo them as new customers. Because a smoker is less likely to inhale cigars, one may suppose them to be harmless, or at least compared to cigarettes, like pea shooters to a cannon.

• • •

This is not to condemn cigars, or cigarettes for that matter. I've enjoyed them both and still may on occasion. Rather, it is to marvel at the merchandising wizardry of the cigar folk.

A few years ago, you began seeing photos of ladies with cigars in delicate hands. Not old ward bosses or redneck deputies but genteel, immaculately groomed females. We were witnessing merchandising masters at their subtle best.

The silk stocking crowd began having "cigar parties." The industry started its own sleek magazine, *Cigar Aficionado,* sponsoring fancy trade shows around the land, with vendors paying $3,000 for booths and customers shelling out $150 to attend and sop up freebies. A recent *New Yorker* had a full-page ad pushing some elite cigar, right along with full pages occupied by Tiffany, Cartier, Remy Martin and the Union Bank of Switzerland. Fancy retailers installed cigar boutiques. You could buy Christmas ties with cigar designs.

Upscale restaurants began including "cigar rooms" for patrons. One new hot spot in New York advertises "100 different cigars" for sale. Last month came the announcement of an international chain of Lone Wolf Cigar Lounges. Heck, nobody ever did this for those evil old low-class scum-bum cigarettes. You never heard of a Snuff Salon, have you?

• • •

The first time I can remember a similar merchandising attack concerned horn-rim glasses. Heretofore, spectacles were designed to be unobtrusive. People with inferior eyesight considered it a mark of weakness, and if they must wear glasses, they wanted them as little noticeable as possible. Rimless things or flesh-colored rims.

Then, near as I can recall, a young actor named Robert Walker wore black horn rims in a movie, playing a romantic lead. Suddenly, horn rims were all over the place. Cary Grant, Phil Silvers, Doris Day, Boris Karloff, Winston Churchill, for goodness sakes. In a matter of months, it seemed, eyeglasses went from stigma to badge.

Modern merchandising? I give you this Tickle Me Elmo or whatever that silly toy currently is the craze.

Over the years, without realizing, I have butted constantly into another crafty form of marketing. As a devout chilihead, I have been exposed to many different recipes for this unique ambrosia. Without exception, all formulas call for chili meat in increments of two pounds. Two pounds, four pounds, six pounds, etc. yet I have never been able to find chili meat in two-pound packages. It's always 1.63 pounds or 1.71 pounds. Why not standardize packages at two pounds? I have mentioned this to butchers and received thoughtful nods in return.

Recently, I was carping on the subject to a weary checkout lady at the supermarket.

THIS AND THAT

"I have never, never found a two-pound package of chili meat," I said crossly. "It's always a pound and a third or some odd figure while recipes always call for two pounds."

"What do you do about it?" the checkout lady said, with no noticeable interest, punching her register.

"Well, I have to buy two packages."

"Aha," she said without expression. Aha indeed.

Advertising Moonshiners Don't Give Up

(*Dallas Morning News,* February 20, 1997)

The first advertising moonshiner I knew personally was Mr. Archibald Moore. His official trade was boxing, but if you weren't careful, he would con you out of your coin purse and the deed to your house.

Mr. Moore was a delightful self-promoter and probably still is active this very day at the age of two redwoods. As he once promised appreciative pressboxers, Mr. Moore intends to live forever or die trying.

It's been maybe 40 years since Mr. Moore climbed into a San Diego ring and slowly turned his stern to the national TV cameras. In big bold letters across the back of his robe was something like: "Sol's Diamond Shop, 2023 Stanhope."

Well, the TV advertising gang choked on their olives. Mr. Moore, canny as any backroads navigator, was moonshining advertising, and the high sheriffs couldn't do a dang thing.

Mr. Moore expressed great amazement at the uproar. "I have a piece of Sol's action," he murmured demurely. "What's to stop me from writing my own business on the back of my robe?"

What indeed? Apparently, the only escape was for TV cameramen to avoid such signs.

• • •

Archie's scam was crude. Hustlers quickly refined the art.

A Midwest appliance outfit would slap a gimme cap, with its logo plainly displayed, on the winner of a televised golf tournament for the award ceremony and interview. If the cameras caught the cap, the golfer got a free refrigerator. Endorsement fees, of course, have since gone to the moon.

When television banned tobacco ads, companies bought signs around stock-car tracks, where cameras were sure to give them glancing exposure. The machines themselves became growling billboards; everywhere a camera pointed, there was a commercial decal infringing on the view.

Promoter Don King, who leaves no soul unturned, painted a beer logo on the ring canvas of televised bouts. Cameramen could hardly avoid it.

When the first O.J. Simpson trial opened, the rear of Judge Lance Ito's computer screen was in constant focus for the fixed TV cameras. The brand name SONY, in big black letters, was prominent. (Someone objected, and the letters were repainted gray but still were legible.)

• • •

Moonshiners love new challenges. Note any NFL quarterback the moment he leaves the field and removes his helmet. An equipment man immediately hands over a gimme cap, plainly emblazoned with the symbol of whatever sport company the player represents.

Is it written in the player's endorsement contract that he wear the cap whenever TV cameras are around?

"Well, it's not in the contract," Troy Aikman said, "but it is strongly recommended."

There was a dandy last week, when the O.J. Simpson damage verdict was announced. CNN cameras were stationed outside the Santa Monica courthouse. In the near background of the two commentators, a fellow carried a huge sign, maybe four by ten feet, with huge, plain letters: "THE VIRGIN MARY SPEAKS TO AMERICA," along with an 800 number to call.

The Simpson verdict came, and camera lights glowed. While the commentators expounded at length, the sign passed in the background slowly, deliberately, back and forth for, oh, maybe 40 minutes. You couldn't escape it; the tenacity was fascinating.

Had the sign advertised a beer or gasoline additive, certainly the fellow would have been chased away. Obviously, no one knew how to treat a distraction with a religious bent. (Incidentally, I dialed the 800 number, and a recording asked for name and address. I passed.)

While reviewing these incidents, a bubble formed above this noble head, a light bulb within. You have noted that every time TV cameras roam the sidelines of any sporting event, the muggers always mouth the same message. Always. You can easily read the lips.

So I intend to market something—fudge, oatmeal, waffle mix—under the name of "Hi Mom." There's a moonshine fortune out there, and I want some.

THIS AND THAT

Survival Is Its Own Reward

(*Dallas Morning News,* October 14, 1999)

The anniversary reminds that modesty finally is sinking in. Ten years ago Sunday, your intrepid correspondent supposedly became a crusty veteran of a memorable earthquake.

To be sure, it was not the first such experience. There had been a cocktail hour in an Acapulco high rise when the chandelier began swinging madly in relation to a distant quake in Mexico City. And there was an afternoon in Los Angeles when I sat in a hotel, composing newspaper prose on a laptop, and a subway train rumbled beneath the Biltmore. Then dawned the realization there was no subway within 3,000 miles.

But now we come to October 17, 1989, and the scene is Candlestick Park in San Francisco. The first two World Series games were played in Oakland, across the bay. Our usual platoon—Nanners Foster of South Carolina, Bugsy Pope of Miami, Mad Dog Murray of LA and Billygoat Millsaps of Richmond—chose to remain in our Oakland motel and commute via rent car to subsequent games in San Francisco.

Now it was five o'clock, and the stadium lights were on. The media horde had quit the field and deposited communication tools in the mezzanine workroom.

• • •

Our bunch was assigned seats in a special press section behind home plate, a splendid view on a comfortable evening. For the benefit of the media's review, there were several TV sets on platforms atop slender posts about eight feet high.

Suddenly, a strange roar sat on the stadium, and the immediate impression was that Navy planes were doing one of those low-level flyovers so common at special events just before action begins. Folks in the right-field stands must have thought likewise because in recognition, they began cheering and doing a "wave."

Then we felt a jerk, like a shark had taken the outrigger bait. Or maybe you were riding atop a placid elephant that suddenly began to tap dance. The TV sets began to jiggle atop their platforms. That, the TV set dance, was when us flatland furriners realized something was awry.

Behind us, an experienced native volunteered, "I'd say that was a pretty good one." He didn't seem alarmed, and most others weren't, although a few jumped up and stumbled down the steps to the nearest exit. Surprisingly few.

Below, players deserted the dugouts, and many had gathered their families from the stands and stood bewildered in infield clumps. Eventually, a calm voice over the p.a. advised people to leave the stadium in an orderly fashion, and, surprisingly enough, they did so. Nobody ran, nobody panicked or called out.

• • •

Maybe an hour later, the power failed, and it was dark, except for flames on the west horizon. Police chased reporters from their emergency work stations in a dim corridor. There may have been structural damage, said they, and everyone must vacate, which we did in a rather ordinary fashion. Rather gallantly, we thought.

Somehow, in a manner reminiscent of the Three Stooges, our bunch somehow found each other in the dark, somehow located the rental car and somehow drove bumper to bumper south, searching for operative telephones. Finally, we found a Bay bridge still operating, one that led us back to Oakland, to a normal, well-lighted, functional, moister world.

Properly nourished, we stayed up the rest of the night, listening to reports of damage and feeling exceedingly heroic. There were 67 fatalities, another thousand injured, a bridge buckled, a freeway collapsed. And a World Series delayed ten days.

We all became doughty earthquake survivors who had

This and That

braved the mighty danger and had not flinched nor cried aloud. Until just recently when we read about the quake in Taiwan, killing more than 1,100 and injuring another 3,500, and one in Turkey, where 16,000 died. And we must finally acknowledge that our experience was embarrassingly bush league and quite fortunately so.

Scene's Beauty Screens Viewer from Reality

(*Dallas Morning News,* August 31, 2000)

This was a weird setting for a tableau. You think of soft lights and a pleasant background for such, and yet here was a miserable August afternoon, with a merciless sun striking and bouncing off Griffiin Street cement. The wind swirled through the downtown canyon as usual, but the swirls were scorching. Not a fitting set for a tableau. Mad dogs and Englishmen, said Noel Coward, go out in the midday sun.

This was no mad dog that caught the eye, but a magnificent creature, an aristocratic presence there on the concrete island, oblivious to the blistering stone beneath his paws, waiting stoically with a patience that bordered on snobbery.

The motorist, waiting at the stoplight, comfortable in his air conditioning, stared in appreciation. This was a short-haired, brindle male, knee high, thick neck, broad of chest. It likely was a boxer, if indeed boxers can have black eyes and muzzle. Other than poodles and cockers, the gawker was no expert on brands, but he was a fan of them all.

This surely was an animal from luxury, well-fed, groomed, mannerly, patient as he waited, even though the pavement was a blast furnace.

* * *

It seemed longer, but it was only a moment or so that the gawker stared at this animal. Just for a split second, their eyes locked, and the human found himself, ridiculously, hoping the animal would see and recognize, perhaps acknowledge, the admiration. But then the dog's dark, sad eyes flicked away. Perhaps he was used to such attention, maybe he was regally uninterested.

(The old gripe returned: If men of science can put a toy car on Mars and transmit photographs of its movement, if they can dig up some pharaoh's bones and decide what he ate for supper 10,000 years ago, surely they could invent some apparatus that could tell what a dog is thinking. Or maybe it's best we don't know?)

This animal's plush surroundings were probably an elegant suite in a downtown hotel. The dog—Bruno surely was his name, he *looked* like a Bruno—spent his morning stretched on the cool tile of the entrance hall, eyes on the door, waiting patiently for his mistress to return and take him out for his daily exercise. Bruno needs a stroll every single day, said the society vet.

• • •

The mistress, casually holding the leash, was equally striking. She wore one of those billowing, flowery silk dresses, which hot gusts occasionally pinned against a long, lithe frame that was obviously, uh, well formed.

The gawker's imagination took over. This surely was a prize model flown in by private jet from New York by the Kim Dawson Agency for a high-toned fashion shoot at Market Hall—$10,000 a day plus a luxury suite and expenses. Ah, that's it. Next week Paris or Barcelona, on a private jet with faithful Bruno curled on a facing lounge. Her pet went almost everywhere with her.

Obviously, she had returned to her downtown hotel suite after four hours under the lights, off with work clothes, on with the flowing silk and sandals and out for a ten-block constitutional for Bruno. Long-striding, carefree and confident was this classic young woman; you sensed it from her breezy dress and casual elegance.

She didn't wear the oversized shades that theatrical young ladies affect. Her face was bare and tanned and turned unfazed to the sun, yellow hair swirling, impervious to the heat.

Obviously, she had seen the gawker's fascination with her dog, and as his focus swung to her, she had looked away, a half-smile on her face, perhaps amused, not surprised but mildly pleased that someone found the tableau so striking. She was accustomed to such attention.

Wait, as the gawker looked at her face, he realized something was wrong with the tableau, drastically wrong. The young lady had not noticed him admiring her handsome escort and was not now aware of his appreciative gaze on her striking self. She didn't see all that because she couldn't.

What Makes a Watermelon Taste Best?

(*Dallas Morning News,* November 14, 2000)

In the supermarket environment, the watermelon looked tasty enough. True, it was just a wedge and wrapped in plastic, which prevented a good old-fashioned shopping sniff. But the color was a hearty red, and the rind was not discolored.

Once it reached the kitchen table, however, the melon had all the flavor of a used paper napkin. And this was sad to a palate that still remembered the taste of a fresh *citrullus vulgaris,* as we used to call it down on the farm.

Of course, that palate has been abused through the years, what with demon rum and tobacco and chili applications. Probably the whole melons found today in farmers markets and in truck beds alongside the road still have that old revered flavor. But not the refrigerated things you find in the vegetable section. You feel for youngsters whose only exposure to the watermelon taste comes from such commercial packaging.

• • •

Watermelons once were very much a part of growing up in this state, back when pleasures were simpler and more rare. Even when times were bad, with cotton prices bottoming and banks foreclosing, the joy of watermelons remained constant, perhaps even gaining in delight because of dismal comparisons. And you could grow watermelons anywhere, even though sandy loam was preferable. Plant the seeds between peach or pecan trees or wherever. Throw them in the air, and they would land and sprout.

(There is still three times more Texas acreage planted in watermelons than any other vegetable. Melons are the state's second-biggest vegetable cash crop behind onions, it says right there in your trusty *Texas Almanac,* published by our very own Belo Corp., a statement instantly recognized as a shameless commercial.)

In those old threadbare days, there was no such evil as refrigeration to sap the natural sweetness. Ideally, you would pull the melon from the vine and cool it in the heavenly waters of a free-flowing spring, back when we had such natural resources. Or tote it home and put it in the icebox until suppertime. Or until Sunday afternoon after the neighborhood ballgame. If you don't know what an icebox is, ask the nearest geezer, if you can find one upright.

Sometimes, in the field, if you were thirsty enough, you would simply lift the melon and let it fall to the ground and crack open. Then, with your fingers, you would grab a handful of the "heart" and gobble it down.

There were always plenty of melons in our little Central Texas hamlet. (I can remember my father buying a whopping 65-pound melon for 65 cents.) Sometimes, the things were so plentiful and cheap they weren't worth hauling into market, so farmers fed them to their hogs, who dearly loved such treatment.

• • •

Of course, there was the traditional belief that stolen watermelons had a better flavor than bought ones, and that was a leading mischief of the day, finding a patch just becoming ripe and sneaking enough for a feast.

There was the parable about the mean old farmer who wearied of having his watermelons stolen by midnight raiders. So he erected a big sign in the patch: ONE OF THESE WATERMELONS HAS BEEN POISONED.

The next morning, he went down to the field and the "One" had been crossed out and "Two" substituted.

One midnight, your hero here instigated a watermelon caper. I told some fellow fuzzcheek miscreants about spotting a vulnerable patch, just coming into ripeness, at the edge of town. We piled into an old flivver and made our midnight raid, handing the prizes through the bobwire fence with expert stealth. Then, we drove to a creek bank and gorged with great satisfaction.

217

Somehow, I had failed to mention that the farm belonged to an uncle who had told me earlier in the week that his watermelon crop was too big and that the melons would rot on the ground and to come help myself. I didn't tell my fellow thieves, lest it diminish the flavor.

Sports

Lords of the Ring, the Field, and Other Venues

Mystery Guests

(*Dallas Times Herald,* December 18, 1981)

From a pressboxer's memorybook:

The sportswriter, in Dallas, picked up his phone. On the other end were a couple of pals in New York, calling from a luncheon table at P. J. Clarke's. One was connected with a sports documentary movie company. His outfit had just finished a highlight film on Cotton Bowl games.

A fledgling actor was flying to Dallas to record an intro and some voice commentary on the film, said ole pal. He was a football fan. In fact, the young actor had played a little college ball in Florida. And he was donating his time and talent to the Cotton Bowl project. He was doing it for expenses only, just for the exposure he might get from the film.

Could the sportswriter do ole pal a favor and fix the actor up with a date in Dallas? Some chick who would show him the sights?

"I'm not in the date business," protested the sportswriter. (I wasn't going to volunteer for social director for some young punk egotist I had never heard of.) "Tell him to go to Old Town. I hear there are some swinging single bars, or whatever you call them."

Later on, I learned that is exactly where Burt Reynolds went, and enjoyed himself quite successfully.

• • •

The sportswriter had been in his room high in the Hotel Americana in Houston, typing his prizefight column. It was after midnight when he finished, and he threw on a jacket and went downstairs to file his copy back to Dallas with Western Union.

There was one person on the elevator when the writer boarded. It happened to be one of the boxers who had won a fight that night. He had knocked out Cleveland Williams, in fact.

"Helluva fight," said the typist. "That's probably the best you've ever looked."

The fighter seemed almost embarrassed. "Do you *really* think so?" he said softly. "That's awfully nice of you to say so." He looked at the writer's jacket. The collar was haphazardly upturned.

"Here, let me fix that," said the fighter. He turned down the collar and patted it gently in place. "There, now you look nice." He smiled and ducked his head and studied his shoes.

Just then the elevator stopped on the mezzanine floor, the doors opened and there was a crowd of fight followers packed outside. Instantly, the quiet, retiring fighter became another personality.

"Ah'm the greatest!" he yelled. "Ah'm Muhammad Ali and ah'm the greatest that ever lived!" The champ raised his arms above his head and marched out into the adoring masses.

• • •

The fuzzy-cheeked sportswriter was on the far outskirts of a table at the old Toots Shor's in New York, where some respected elders were gathered. One had just finished a book and the others were wishing him a successful market.

"Oh, it doesn't have a chance," said Bob Considine. "The only four-letter words in it are Babe and Ruth."

• • •

Some promotional brain came up with a gimmick for the Texas League, which was beginning to struggle a bit after a flush of postwar prosperity.

There would be a beauty contest to elect Miss Texas League. Each of the eight member cities would be represented by a local beauty and the troupe would be sent around to appear at each ballpark. The fans would vote at each park; the ballots would be tabulated. And the winner would make public appearances for the league for the next few months.

The girls would be presented in bathing suits, of course,

and they were strictly chaperoned by a matron and an advertising guy who accompanied the beauties around the league.

After the tour was half completed, the ad guy confided: "There may be prettier gals on the tour, but that Miss Houston will win it. She does the most with what she has. She's a bright one and, buddy, she knows what she wants."

The perky Miss Houston became Miss Texas League alrighty, and then stepped off to Hollywood and changed her name from Grandstaff to Grant and finally to Mrs. Bing Crosby.

• • •

The sportswriter-to-be was then a sailor on shore leave in Los Angeles, just before a wartime Christmas. A shipmate had been a Wabash College roommate of a chap named Steve Crane, who was then married to Lana Turner.

Crane had some Christmas shopping and errands to run one day, and he took the two sailors along. One stop was a barber shop above a haberdashery in Beverly Hills. Rothschild's was the name? Or something similar.

In the chair next to Crane was a husky, well-groomed guy, slick dark hair parted in the middle like Richard Barthelmess. Crane introduced the sailors to the guy, Bennie Something Or Other. He was robustly friendly. He had a son, he said, in the Air Force in England. If there was anything he could do for the sailors while they were on leave, anything at all, please let him know. He shook hands goodbye and repeated the offer.

Downstairs, in the car, Crane asked: "Do you know who that was?"

No. Bennie Something Or Other. Some nice middle-aged guy with a son in the Air Force.

"It was Bennie Siegel," said the host. "They call him Bugsy. Bugsy Siegel. Maybe you've heard of Murder Incorporated?"

Olympics Buffs

(Dallas Morning News, July 18, 1996)

Some of the boys at the pool hall heard tell that our fine Olympic athletes were going around nekkid as a jaybird. Naturally, being young and impressionable, they were interested in pursuing the subject, or perhaps pursue is not the proper verb.

Anyways, they wondered what the world was coming to if our stalwarts were parading without clothes and having their pictures took.

Well, a bit of research by your dispassionate agent quieted the lads. It seems that a dozen or so of the Yanks—including Carl Lewis, Michael Johnson and Jackie Joyner-Kersee—had indeed peeled to the hide for a *Life* magazine photographer. But they were "strategically posed," as the saying goes, so that the human body could be celebrated without fear it would wind up on the sex channel or sent through the post in an unmarked envelope.

However, as I told the curious younguns, it would hardly be an Olympic first if some folks appeared in the altogether. In early Olympic days, it was not only fashionable to appear in the nude but required.

• • •

Of course, this is going back even before Bob Dole was born. Some big shots named Cleosthenes, Lycurgus and Iphitus decided it was time their subjects in Sparta, Pisa and Elis took time off from whopping each other with war clubs and played some gentler games. So they decided to get together in a nearby pasture and throw something called a discus, the second most popular pastime behind sticking each other with javelins. This was back around 776 B.C., so long ago women's lib hadn't been invented.

In fact, the first Olympic games were for men only. The

females couldn't even buy a ticket in the bleachers. Sometimes, curiosity would overcome a lady and she would shinny up a nearby tree or hide behind a hedge to watch her ever-loving boyfriend run or jump or throw things. If these peepers were caught in the spying act, they were liable to be struck with a small ax. To be sure, it was an offense punishable by death in the first degree.

One year, a lady name Phernice had a son named Peisidorous, who was a fisticuffer in the Olympics. Showing motherly concern plus typical female curiosity, Ms. Phernice was determined to tend her son. So she dressed in men's clothes, balled up her hair with bobby pins and passed herself off as her son's male trainer. However, after Peisidorous put the clobber on his opponent, Ms. Phernice forgot her role and hugged and kissed her victorious offspring.

The Olympic sheriffs did a double take, figuring right away that this was no way for one fellow to act toward another fellow. (I *told* you this was a long time ago!) So the guards grabbed the suspect and determined, probably by the scent of her perfume, that Phernice was a female type, and she was put on trial for her life.

Ms. Phernice pleaded motherhood and got a suspended sentence. But she was responsible for a new Olympic rule. From that point on, trainers were ordered to appear in the nude. This was a source of some embarrassment.

• • •

The Greek mothers finally rebelled against the boycott. They went next door in another pasture and staged some athletic events of their very own, throwing skillets and such. This competition was called the Heraca Games, and they were held every four years, same as the Olympics.

Finally, the menfolk wearied of their housemates being gone so much, out somewhere running relays and throwing spears and leaving them home with TV dinners. So they relented and allowed the ladies to spectate and even buy seats in the luxury boxes. And the trainers were ordered to put their breeches back on, which came as a great relief to these gents because this was before the day of sunblock.

At any rate, nudity is not new to the Olympics, and it would not be shocking one of these days if it returned to the games themselves—competitors, trainers, spectators, media, beer vendors and even Mr. Bob Costas, all running around in their birthday suits. The calculated result will send the price of TV rights right through the roof. Unless, of course, the shoe sponsors rebel, arguing that their products were hardly noticed anymore.

Swimmers Also Dredge for Cash

(*Dallas Morning News,* June 5, 1997)

It may strike you that every time you look up, some citizen is swimming from here to yonder, by his own choice. The reasons behind such ventures may be foreign to us common blokes, but there is no accounting for tastes. Frederick the Great, history tells us, put mustard in his coffee.

It has long been the premise here that one swims long distances only when pursued by something with sharp teeth. But frequently some person arrives with an artistic reason. Such as this Ms. Susie Maroney, who recently swam from Cuba to Florida when she didn't have to.

Ms. Maroney did her act inside a metal cage the size of a house trailer to shield her from curious monsters. Under these conditions, we assume the shark hierarchy will scoff at this record, bringing up an interesting point. Her feat took 24 hours and 34 minutes, but the absence of a shark cage might have inspired her to swim much faster. It would me.

• • •

The 112-mile trip was made more difficult, said Ms. Maroney, by jellyfish slipping inside the cage and stinging her bare flesh. But even this was not as distasteful as a swim around Manhattan Island three years ago, when she kept bumping into dead bodies, such as rats and people.

Obviously, Ms. Maroney intends to make a career out of such feats and now hopes to swim from Cuba to Mexico, a space of 140 miles. It isn't clear where the profit is in these endeavors, but you may assume there is some.

It hasn't been long since a Frenchman named Guy Delage claimed to have swum the whole dang Atlantic. Took him 55 days, from Cape Verde to Barbados. But he had detractors who sneered at his claim because he frequently rested on a raft he was towing, which had food, drink, a radio and a fax machine.

That's right, a fax machine. Dang things are taking over the Earth. I got attacked by one in a parking lot the other day.

• • •

Speaking of commercialism, there was my favorite swimmer ever, the illustrious Fred Baldasare, who aspired to swim the English Channel *underwater* almost four decades ago. Our man not only beseeched the public for donations but wrote his own press releases. His compositions were classic.

In these remarkable bulletins, Mr. Baldasare always referred to himself in the third person.

"A fine athlete, he won medals as a gymnast and boxed professionally. His boxing career was terminated by his induction into the armed forces," clacked his muscular typewriter. "After breaking his back, he was honorably discharged and sought a career as a photographer's model. Because of his good looks and fine physique, he was soon on the covers of magazines."

One Channel attempt failed, he wrote, because of a lack of sleep due to "the heavy demands of the many journalists covering his deed." Another time, he was betrayed by a British assistant who was "cutting up with a French girl" and "later found to be drunk." Once he was dragged from the water, he wrote, with "his incredibly well-trained legs threshing, beating the surface to a froth."

Mr. Baldasare's pleas for donations often expressed panic. He warned that a Russian was preparing for a similar attempt. "He is supposedly subsidized by his government," wrote our man. "It would be unfortunate if this would happen when Mr. Baldasare, who pioneered this swim, could capture the honors for his country of which he is immensely fond."

In training for another Channel effort, Mr. Baldasare wrote that he would swim completely around the island of Sicily.

"He will spear fish as he goes along," wrote himself. "This will give him an objective to offset the deadly monotony of training. Fish that he will spear, amounting to thousands of pounds, will be given to the needy as he circles the island. This will be much appreciated by the people concerned."

Such unselfish projects must have stimulated donators. Mr. Baldasare found financial backers and did his underwater number, from Calais to the White Cliffs. Then he told reporters he planned to become a movie star. From there, his trail disappears, but he was sorely missed not only by hungry folk on the Sicilian coast but by literature as a whole, which his incredibly well-trained ego beat to a froth.

Top Athlete? For Me It Is No Contest

(*Dallas Morning News,* July 22, 1999)

Like every ink-stained wretch still able to sit up and take nourishment, your resident geezer here voted in several of those century-end polls. This is much the rage nowadays before 2000, when that Y2K thing turns us all into pumpkins.

Some New York outfit, on a TV project, requested a ranking of the top 50 athletes of the century. In a suspense technique that would turn Agatha Christie green as a tree lizard, the network then dribbles the results in deliberate doses, calculated to keep sports nuts on their tippy-toes. The Supreme Jock won't be revealed until Dec. 26, at which time the world will stand still, no forelock untugged.

Joe Fan could presume the No. 1 choice will be Michael Jordan, the sneaker salesman who dabbled in basketball. Or maybe Babe Ruth, the baseball legend, or Muhammad Ali. My stubborn vote went elsewhere.

• • •

Several ensuing months have dimmed memory, but I do recall my first two picks. Mostly, it came down to definition.

To this voter, Athlete of the 20th Century means a person with a variety of physical talents. Random House defines athlete as "one trained to compete in contests involving physical agility, stamina and strength." Mind you, the definition says contests—plural.

So for No 2, the choice here was Mildred Babe Didrikson, the Texan excelling in almost any sport she tried. She started as a Beaumont basketballer and moved to a Dallas team that won three national AAU titles.

In the 1932 Olympics at Los Angeles, women were limited to three events; Babe won the javelin and the hurdles and tied for the high jump. The first time on a golf course, she went around in 95 strokes and became the focal point of the first women's professional tournaments. She played softball, volleyball and pool, pitched exhibition games against major leaguers like Jimmy Foxx and beat Ted Williams and Jack Sharkey in their hobby, fly-casting. All of this and much more before she died at 43.

· · ·

This vote for the Century's Top Jock went to Jim Thorpe, perhaps prejudicially because of his shamefully persecuted heritage. Thorpe had Irish blood from a half-breed father but was mostly Sac and Fox, yet another tribe driven from lush Illinois homelands by the new white Americans. Thorpe was born in a shabby cabin in Oklahoma.

At tiny Carlisle Indian Institute in Pennsylvania, which he attended spasmodically, Thorpe did all things football—tackle, block, run, pass, catch and kick. Against West Point (a squad member was named Dwight Eisenhower), the fleet Thorpe returned a kickoff 90 yards only to have the touchdown called back on a penalty. The second kickoff, Thorpe returned 95 yards and told the referee, "185 yards is a long way to run for a score."

In the 1912 Olympics at Stockholm, he won both the decathlon and pentathlon, which was unprecedented, only to have his medals later recalled because it was discovered, as John Lardner wrote, "he once played a semi-pro baseball game for 35 cents and a jar of buttermilk."

He played pro football until he was 41 and spent six seasons in the Giants' outfield. He would win a pool game and jump flat-footed over the table. He won a national intercollegiate ballroom dancing contest. Name it, he did it better than you.

In later years, he also could drink more firewater than you and worked at everything from a gate guard and ditch digger to a movie bit player and carnival attraction. He died in a California trailer park, large, mellow and good-natured. He never mentioned Stockholm.

After his death, Olympic nabobs returned his medals to his

family. In an earlier poll, Thorpe was voted top athlete of the half-century, leading Mr. Lardner to comment: "All in all, it is nice to see Mr. Thorpe get in his due in the 1950 poll. A further move to give the country back to his people was defeated by several votes."

Dinosaurs Once Ruled Sportsdom

(Dallas Morning News, May 25, 2000)

It was the American statesman Ted Williams' first spring as a Texas Ranger manager, and he made a rare appearance at the press' motel work room in Pompano Beach, Fla.

This was not a favorite chore with Mr. Williams. Most reporters, in his opinion, lived in a hole and waited for something to die or get hurt. But this night, he was feeling benevolent after a supper of fried chicken (he usually ate seven pieces at a sitting), and the Rangers' road secretary- diplomat Burt Hawkins persuaded him to visit the leper camp.

Ted had his hearing impaired as a Marine combat pilot and, as a weird compensation, spoke with considerable volume. Walls quivered. Venetian blinds clattered. Reporters quaked, and their ice cubes clanked.

Mr. Williams is a blunt fellow of strong opinions, which on this rare night, he delivered on a variety of subjects, making generous use of exclamation points. His favorite U.S. president was Herbert Hoover! Ezzard Charles was the greatest heavyweight champ!

When the Rangers still were located in Washington, Mr. Williams had met Vince Lombardi, who had just taken over the Redskins.

"Greatest football coach ever lived!" Announced Mr. Williams. "He won't take no guff from nobody, not press, not players, not officials, not owners, nobody! He tells a player to run through a wall, by God, the player better do it or else!"

A reporter cleared his nervous throat and offered a mild prediction: The way things are going, in a couple of years, if Mr. Lombardi tries that stuff, his players will walk out.

"What!" Mr. Williams stabbed the poor man with a vicious glare while he searched for volume.

"By God . . ." and then he looked down at the motel carpeting. "I expect you're right." The thought seemed to depress him, and shortly after, he went to his room.

• • •

That's generally the reaction from the geezer bleachers when a basketball coach was publicly rapped for roughhouse tactics, physical and oral. Bob Knight, the resident ogre at Indiana, was put on a short leash by the college president, who clearly would rather have been wading naked in the Amazon, trying to catch piranhas in a tablespoon.

For years, Bob Knight has run the tightest of operations at Indiana, loud, overbearing, dictatorial, occasionally shoving or pushing a player and using language that would peel paint off a piano. Incidentally, he also insisted players attend classes and graduate and refrain from attacking coeds in dormitory rooms. Old-fashioned rascal.

Even in the face of changing times, Mr. Knight stuck to his old guns, and his teams were so successful, the game remained a religion in his state and he became the patron saint. Of course, at the time of Mr. Knight's setdown, you heard trustee president John Walda say, "There are no sacred cows at Indiana University, and that certainly includes the basketball coach."

This may have been the funniest line since Groucho Marx.

Of course, the reason public censure now is slapped on the coach is that his teams haven't been playoff prominent of late. In his state and on his campus, that was Mr. Knight's greatest crime. Not his tactics, his record.

• • •

As for his treatment of players, Mr. Knight would be laughed out of Marine boot camp. Old-timers will remember dictators who would put Mr. Knight to shame—names like Neyland, Bryant, Hayes and Rupp. Take the old Texas Tech football taskmaster Pet Cawthon, who might send his squad to bed without supper. Or, if he didn't like a game performance, might march his players back on the field and hold a fierce scrimmage.

BLACKIE SHERROD AT LARGE

There was never a schoolboy, especially in this state, who hasn't seen a teammate jerked around by his helmet strap in practice or booted in the pants when he lined up wrong.

Bob Knight's most grievous fault, it says here from years around the guy, was bullydom. He was, and probably still is, a shameful physical and mental bully to those weaker than he. The best cure for a bully is to meet a bigger bully, and sooner or later, it usually happens.

Winter Games Once Were No Big Deal

(*Dallas Morning News,* February 14, 2002)

For the past week, unless you have been in a convenient coma, you have been beaten about the head and shoulders with the Winter Olympics.

You may not know a luge from a chocolate malt, but it is not from a lack of exposure, both in the public prints and, mostly, on the boob toob. We are up to our armpits in the triple Lutz and clap skates. We know what size boots were worn by the grandpa of Irina Slutskaya back in Moscow and how many beets she prefers on her breakfast cereal.

We are bombarded with photographed glories of the great outdoors around Salt Lake City. Somehow faded into the background are the bribery scandal that preceded these Games and the grave concern of insufficient saloons in the Mormon country to serve the international gullets. Thank goodness, we got that settled. The visitors have been assured there are 1,305 places to drink within reach of the Olympic areas. To put this in perspective, this is twice as many as in Lillehammer and Nagano put together, surely a statistic for Olympic chronicles and enough to make America proud.

However, with all this attention and exposure, it wasn't always thus, and this brings us to our text for today. About time.

• • •

Four decades ago, the Winter Olympics had never been on television. In truth, the Summer Games had received only periodic reports on the newscasts. The Winter Olympics, who cared. Look it up in the agate print of your sports page.

But in the New York offices of CBS, a young assistant sports director had a silly idea. The 1960 Winter Games were scheduled for Squaw Valley, and our man wondered why the network didn't shoot for the moon and televise the events as one big show, not just an afterthought on daily newscasts.

It was a hard sell. CBS bosses looked at the young man warily and considered calling for the white coats. The suits decided against the grandiose plans and, in fact, surrendered the rights to rival ABC, which studied the proposition and said no thanks. Finally, the CBS brass folded and told our hero it was his baby, and heaven help him if it flopped.

Our pioneer spent two years on the project, making a couple of dozen trips to California, living in a motel room and dogging the surveyors as they plotted the ski courses. He blazed trees and marked rocks where cameras could best be located. He wanted to sink the cables in the summer, before snow and ice made digging difficult. He hired a handful of workers and trudged mountainsides as they unrolled the big cable spools.

Mind you, this was in 1959, shortly after Columbus discovered America, and such an expansive project ranked right up there with Fulton's Folly. Our guy wanted to show all events at their sites and have a commentator on hand (he even hired former gold medalists like Dick Button to handle the expertise). He stole an idea from political convention coverage and established a main news desk and persuaded a fellow named Walter Cronkite to serve as anchor.

At the most, the pioneer had 100 workers, where NBC now has 10 times as many. Also, NBC paid $545 million for these TV rights today, whereas CBS got them for free in 1960, although the network did contribute something like $15,000 to the Olympic fund.

• • •

That revolutionary Squaw Valley project was a huge success—18 hours of prime-time exposure, and the ratings went to the moon. The innovator became a hero on Madison Avenue and was offered all sorts of promotions and propositions. NBC tried to hire him to run its coverage of the upcoming Summer Games in Rome.

But our man already had a job. During his two years of planning and executing the revolutionary project in Squaw

237

Valley, he had decided to return to his first love. He had been contacted about launching a professional football franchise in Texas for a wealthy young man named Murchison. So, for the next 30 years, Tex Schramm ran the Dallas Cowboys.

The Big, Wide World

War, Espionage, and Similar Issues of Global Importance

O'Grady Makes Us Remember What True Heroes Are Like

(Dallas Morning News, June 22, 1995)

Capt. Scott O'Grady, bless his hide, is beneficiary of an ancient law of nature. Timing is everything.

First gent to make this observation, to the best of my research, was a Greek poet entitled Hesiod, a part-time shepherd who went through life without a first name.

"Observe due measure," wrote Mr. Hesiod, "for right timing is in all things the most important factor."

Capt. O'Grady came along when the nation was crying out for a hero. We had run out. In traditional interpretation, heroes are wartime products and we ain't had any fully grown wars lately. One-sided "police actions" don't qualify.

At any rate, Capt. O'Grady's aircraft was shot down by a Bosnian Serb missile, and for six days he kept his wits and survived in hostile hills until our lads staged a dramatic rescue. In old days of Pacific, Korea and Vietnam campaigns, there might be a dozen such adventures every week, or perhaps every day. But we have had none lately, and therefore we had a lot of hero worship stacked up.

The trouble with a hero drouth is that we are prone to dip into the recognition stockpile and squander some on people who can hit a ball farther than normal or jump higher or make more money. This is a shameful waste; Capt. O'Grady was a hero of the traditional mode, and we have made the most of it.

The Marine even looks the part, a tough little pine cone with clear eyes and a good cut of jaw. This is not always the case with heroes.

• • •

There's the probability that most of us have crossed trails with Heroes and failed to identify same. They come in a vast assortment of trappings.

241

Whenever I see the word, I think of a nondescript sailor of Pacific days who looked as much the part as Woody Allen. Average size, average hair, features, build, easily lost in a crowd. He was a loner, a Midwest farm boy, silent and solemn, never entering the usual sailor rowdiness.

He was a torpedo plane gunner, and there was one trait that distinguished him from two dozen others in his squadron. The lad got horribly airsick. This was not the ideal situation for his assignment because torpedo planes, given the nature of their employment, weren't noted for smooth trips.

Once his TBF left the flight deck, his stomach began churning, and by the time the plane reached its formation altitude, the poor lad was upchucking to beat the band. Every mission, the same indelicate seizure. Once his painful spasm passed, he settled down and went about his business.

The fellow never mentioned his affliction. The turret gunner in his plane knew, of course. He told other flight crewmen but they discussed it only among themselves. Normally, this would call for a great deal of joshing. But somehow, in this case, no one commented.

The boy could have gone to the flight surgeon and been relieved from flying status and shunted to less stressful duty, at least to a post at sea level. These transfers, for whatever reason, were not uncommon.

However, this particular lad refused even to acknowledge his handicap. Too proud, too embarrassed, too stubborn, too dumb, too frightened, too something. He even went to considerable trouble to hide his ailment. He wore a helmet, of course, but carried his sailor hat, one of those silly white bonnets, in his flight suit pocket. He used it, excuse the expression, as a barf bag.

He was very neat about it. He would secure the cap top with a string and once back aboard ship, he would smuggle the makeshift bag to the nearest bathroom and empty it. Then he would tie a line to the cap, drop it over the side and let the ship tow it through salt water. In minutes, he had a clean receptacle for his next flight. It was a regular chore for him, and soon his peers found other topics to discuss.

One day, of course, his plane didn't make it back to the carrier. All things considered, he might have been the most heroic character I ever came across, and I can't even remember his name.

A Sense of Humor Helps

(*Dallas Morning News,* March 26, 1996)

You know it now as Taiwan, and it is very much in the news. China's bosses threaten to storm its beaches unless the divorced island returns to the mainland fold. U.S. warships cruise the waters, chip on shoulder.

But Taiwan also had intrigue when the island was known as Formosa. A half-century ago, it was under Japanese rule, a bristling advance base of wartime operation.

In August 1945, a puny U.S. task force of two jeep carriers and destoyer escorts sailed northwest from Saipan to attempt the liberation of prisoners of war believed held on Formosa. The operation was experimental; no one could remember a POW liberation without the benefit of ground forces.

There was a hitch. Japan had surrendered only a couple days before, and there was no assurance that word had reached Formosa. This could present an awkward problem because the Formosa troops had considerable firepower and wouldn't take kindly to the U.S. Navy sailing into their front yard without a search warrant.

So the Navy bosses got cute.

They could launch about 50 planes off the two small carriers. The scheme was to fool the Japanese into thinking there were many carriers just beyond the horizon. Pilots were instructed to buzz the island, fly ten miles away, turn and buzz it again, so that it would seem the entire U.S. Navy was approaching with at least a million warplanes loaded and cocked.

• • •

This was a fancy trick but unnecessary. The Formosa forces had indeed learned of the armistice and seemed rather happy about it. A destroyer pushed up a river and moored right in the middle of some town. The prisoners were easily found.

Almost 500 wretches, mostly British, were brought to the carriers. On the open well deck, they were stripped, hosed down and sprayed with de-lousing formula. Heads and body hair were shaved by barbers wearing disinfectant masks. It was demeaning to the poor chaps but necessary. Many were ill with dysentery, pellagra and malnutrition. Their sores were cleansed and treated. They were given new white T-shirts, khaki pants, Army cots and ice cream.

Most were gaunt and silent, with vacant eyes. But one was delightful. He weighed 90 pounds, his collarbone looked like a coat hanger, and most of his teeth were gone. He was in his mid-20s and looked 60, but, golly, what a sense of humor. He immediately latched onto a sympathetic U.S. ear, and he couldn't stop talking. Babbling, actually, for days. But he managed a humorous twist to every story, as tragic as they seemed to his listener. It was as if the lad had discovered that a sense of humor was as vital to survival as oxygen, even through the cruel rigors of man's inhumanity to man.

This chap was a private in the Scottish Black Watch, a storied fierce regiment that, since the 1700s, had worn traditional kilts on battlefields. The Germans called them "the ladies from hell." He was taken at Singapore and had spent four years in POW camps, the last 30 months in the potash mines of Formosa. Potassium nitrate, if you remember your high school chemistry, is a component of explosives, which the Japanese had use for from time to time.

• • •

To wile away his captivity—and perhaps preserve his sanity—this prisoner began nightly work on a slab of heavy hard wood. With a smuggled screwdriver as his only tool, he had painstakingly gouged the insignia of the Black Watch in amazing detail. He recalled every facet of the design and stained the wood with potash and water. Over his 30 months in Formosa stockades, he had forged three of these plaques, and, along with beriberi and tuberculosis, they were all he had to show for his war.

245

Still, a couple days later, as the carrier neared Manila and his berth on a hospital ship, the prisoner untied his pitiful rag bundle and insisted on giving his American friend one of the plaques. The sailor refused. It was too personal. The prisoner penciled his name on the back—"A. Thennington, POW, Formosa, 1942-45"—and threatened to throw it in the sea if his new friend didn't accept it.

The plaque, in its dogged crudeness, has an honest and dignified beauty to it and, to collectors of such mementos, is probably worth a pretty penny. For a half-century, it has hung on my office wall, and it ain't for sale.

Television Can't Tell All about War

(Dallas Morning News, May 6, 1999)

The comparison before the house is between Vietnam and the Balkans, beyond the fact that both are out of town.

The Addled Majority may rate the two "wars" in the same category, finding similarity in that:

1) The United States is sticking its nose in somebody else's fight.

2) Beltway brains underestimated the resolve of the opposition.

3) Even if you triumph, how long do you stay triumphant?

4) The involvement will cost us a ton, a no-win proposition for all U.S. citizens except airplane and munition manufacturers.

This may seem a heartless summation, given the pitiful images on your TV screen of Kosovo mothers, babies and oldsters huddled in scruffy bivouacs, driven by Serb bullies and grieving for relatives and homes lost to neighbors of another religion.

Those electronic relays, to the American mind anyway, seem the most influential phase of this Balkans mess. It also would be so in Rwanda, Ethiopia or wherever intramural war wages and U.S. troops and TV cameras follow.

• • •

This Kosovo business, to us in the balcony, is a television war. Even more than Vietnam, which was the video introduction of warfare to this country. Even more than that vague business in Iraq when Gen. Norman Schwarzkopf regularly filled your screen, grimly garbed in fatigues, sleeves rolled up, chin thrust out, describing how Saddam Hussein would be torn limb from limb by our gallant men and women in the field. And there were the CNN boys manning mikes on rooftops while SCUD missiles and flak streaked the dark sky as a backdrop. Steven Spielberg turned green.

To viewers in this country, wartime has become made-to-order programming, Dan, Tom and Peter in their trusty bush jackets, posing in front of dusty tanks in some forsaken land. The other night, there was Geraldo, flat on his face on an Albanian trail, dodging incoming mortars, he said. (Leading one to wonder why the cameraman also wasn't flat on his face.)

What police action was it, Grenada or where, when invading forces had an awkward time wading ashore because of the strobe lights of news cameramen who had preceded them?

Stephen Ambrose, the esteemed historian of World War II, said recently, "If we had television at the Battle of the Bulge, and American people saw American soldiers lying dead there in the snow, there's a good chance most Americans would say to hell with it, let Hitler have Europe."

That may be stretching a bit, but war television does hold us captive and fascinated. We watch these scenes with great interest, pausing only to go to the fridge, and shake heads sadly at the horror of it all before we yawn comfortably and go to bed on clean sheets.

• • •

In reality, 98 percent of Americans have no idea what war is.

Oh, we think we do, because of what the White House tells us and the bemedaled generals there in daily briefings, pointing at maps and showing filmed missile hits right there on target, by gum. But U.S. citizens can't associate with real war.

War is not standing in line for sugar rations or getting only three gallons of gasoline a week or making do with half-soled shoes and meatless Tuesdays or even, perish forbid, putting a gold star in the window.

Talk to the Brits about what war is. Not to the military; war is its business. But talk to the ordinary bloke; war is huddling the night in a subway while bombs shake above and returning to a home collapsed in rubble and a sister missing and somebody's arm poking from a pile of bricks.

Talk to the Russians and, yes, the Berliners. You can't actually know, really know, war until you feel the shock waves of the bombs, until the flash burns off your eyelashes, until the invading trooper prods your shoulder blade with a bayonet. Television, for all of its remarkable achievements, can't handle that. Not yet.

What If We Were to Drop False Clues?

(*Dallas Morning News,* June 3, 1999)

As all backstretch historians know, the Whitneys and Vanderbilts and Hancocks raised their own racehorses. So did the Phipps family and the Woodwards and Riddles and Wrights. Bred their own stallions to their own mares, by golly, midwifed the births, fed, nurtured, doctored, worried and culled, and maybe one in a dozen made it to the starting gate.

Once in a backstretch chat at Churchill Downs, the question was put to D. Wayne Lukas, then the most successful trainer in the land. Why don't you breed and raise your own horses instead of buying them at yearling auctions?

"Why should I go through all that grief?" said Mr. Lukas. "Let somebody else go to that trouble and worry and expense and heartbreak. When they come up with a product, then I buy it."

• • •

Well, sire, I do not know if Mr. Lukas is a student of Chinese philosophy, although I would not put it past the rascal. But his modus operandi sounds mighty like the Chinese theory on nuclear development.

Our gallant physicists, scourged to their test tubes and charts and computers and technology, worked their foreheads to the bone to find the most effective way of blowing countrysides to small bits. They waded through years of countless details and experiments, discarding this and that, spending money like it was going out of style. The lights burned late in their laboratories. Nobody knows the trouble they seen.

Then, after our physicists have perfected all these witchcrafts, the Chinese communists send some folks over to infiltrate and steal the procedures from under our nonchalant noses. Presto, they have the finished technology, with no costly experiments, no delaying failures, no accidents, no frustrations, no expenses. Just a nice, clean, finished product, wiped clean of fingerprints.

The Chinese philosophers had a saying: *One family builds the wall—two families enjoy it.*

In the meantime, over the space of two decades, the Asians were bowing and smiling and pouring tea and treating U.S. visitors like reverent celebrities.

The Chinese have a saying: *If you want your dinner, don't insult the cook.*

Especially, dating back to the Nixon days, was the bowing and scraping pointed our way.

The Chinese have a saying: *Looking for fish? Don't climb a tree.*

Although of similar political bent, they didn't seem so buddy-buddy with other communist countries, like Russia or Cuba or whatever. Maybe because those folks didn't have anything the Chinese wanted at the moment.

They have a saying: *Do not try to borrow combs from shaven monks.*

• • •

For years, we Yank commoners sorta ignored China despite its population and resources. Actually, the Chinese seemed too busy simply *existing* to make trouble for anybody except their own folks.

A half-century ago, Will Rogers wrote: "China, by far, is the smartest nation in the world."

It should be no surprise that the smartest fellows in the world would let someone else go to the expense and efforts and trials and errors to develop something, then simply swipe the plans. What could be cannier than that? Maybe the reason the Chinese wear those big loose sleeves is so they can laugh up them easier.

Probably John LeCarre or Graham Greene or some spycraft author could dream up something slyer. We have used false codes and dropped false clues during wars, haven't we? What if we planted false secrets, wrong formulas, flawed technology and such, and let the spies steal them and have the dang things blow up in their faces?

Naw, we couldn't be that smart. Might make a good novel and movie, though. Hand me that quill and foolscap, boy, afore I tan your hide. Might as well make a million dollars before the word gets around.

From World Policeman to Keystone Kop

(Dallas Morning News, November 16, 2000)

Just recently, when one of our billion-dollar properties was severely ruptured by two guys in overalls and a rubber boat, Uncle Sam got another jolt. It was like a chump picking up a live wire for the umpteenth time, just to see if it was still juicy.

The question seemed to be: Why would one of our costly craft stop for fuel in such an unfriendly atmosphere as Yemen? It was like leaving your limo in the boondocks, keys in the ignition.

The official explanation was that Yemen was no more dangerous for U.S. representatives than any other port in that part of the world. What the brass hats seem to be saying is, hey, we got enemies everywhere.

Once again we were reminded that we ain't the most popular kid on the block. The Ugly American still lives. Face it, in many foreign locales, while we're handing out free cornmeal, someone is stealing hubcaps off our welcome wagon.

It's enough to make geezers wish to bring our fleet and troops home, build a fence around our borders, drill for necessary oil in Alaska, make our own cameras and T-shirts in our own factories, spend all those foreign-aid billions on our own slums and schools and hospitals, paddle our own dadgum canoe and let the rest of the world go by.

This is juvenile thinking and inhumane and all that bad stuff, but be honest, it does occasionally cross the layman's mind. Especially when some wild eye blows a hole in the USS *Cole* or bombs our embassy in Kenya or Tanzania.

• • •

However, through no intent of our own, perhaps we have found the secret to worldwide compatibility.

Everybody loves a good laugh, and goodness knows, in our presidential election stumbles, we have furnished the international audience with some side splitters. And this may be good. It's awkward to slug someone when you're laughing at him. See a guy slip on a banana peel, you don't run over and bust him in the chops. You're too busy holding your sides.

Remember, we're the hoity-toity folks who chuckle when some Third World nation has a monumental foul-up at the polls. That's really funny to us, those poor souls trying to act like a democracy. Heck, we even send do-gooders, Jimmy Carter and such, over to their poor backward countries to teach them how to run an honest, efficient election. Hey, that's the Christian way, sharing our superior knowledge. Good on us.

Now, in a remarkable change of pace, we give an imitation of a cub bear on ice skates.

• • •

Can you hear the international critics? Pardon moi, are these the intellectuals who would tell us how to restructure our democracy? Balance our budgets? Tote our bales? Who's running their show, Woody Allen?

("If I wrote a script like this," said comedian Rob Reiner, "they'd throw me out of the Screenwriters Guild.")

Did you catch those Yanks on the telly, the *experts,* the *pundits,* fumbling around with their exit polls? Was it a Larry, Curly and Moe rerun? Really, you can't get upset at those Yanks. They're trying to bring back vaudeville.

Hey, comrades, did you hear the routine where one candidate calls to congratulate the other and then, an hour later, calls back to cancel his good wishes? Was that Al Gore or Bob Hope? Hoo, boy, we can't wait until their new president shows up at the next NATO meeting and we can hit him over the head with pig bladders.

They keep recounting Florida ballot boxes, with computers yet, and get new totals each time. Hey, Boris, call Deng, see if he's got an old abacus around there somewhere.

These are not Ugly Americans anymore, they're the Marx

Brothers. You can't be envious of those guys, bless their hearts. We have met the enemy, and he is one of us.

Listen to the Yank historian Daniel Schorr: "We are the laughingstock around the world."

Maybe that ain't all bad. Compassion through comedy. Peace through pratfall. Has a nice ring to it.

Espionage Becomes Confusing

(*Dallas Morning News,* April 12, 2001)

The problem is embarrassing to admit, but we of the Great Unwashed just don't comprehend modern spycraft. They keep changing the dang perimeters.

It was simple enough when Mata Hari, played by Greta Garbo, batted her eyes at the handsome Yank lieutenant, played by Ramon Navarro, until he revealed the number of troops in his regiment. We can understand that, especially when the mademoiselle let the sucker sip champagne out of her slipper, which, we were told, was the size of a bedpan.

Spying was much simpler, dating back to when Moses sent a dozen secret agents into Canaan to scout the Promised Land. After 40 days, they came back with reports of milk and honey and tough guys.

At any rate, the hoi polloi stayed fairly well up on espionage during the Great Hate, with the enemy intercepting and solving our coded wireless messages and vice versa. We could dig it.

Then, in the European war aftermath, when our cagey lads from Langley matched wits with the cagey folks from the KGB, we understood the drama. Remember, there was that trick umbrella with which a Russian assassin jabbed Georgi Markov as he waited for a London bus, injecting him with *ricin,* which, as any fool knows, is a poison made of castor oil seeds. Believe me, we knew something about castor oil.

• • •

But when the spy stuff moved upstairs, it lost us commonfolk. Star Wars took over.

Forty years ago, when an American aviator, Francis Gary Powers, was shot down by the Russkies, he was flying something called a U2, which was way high taking pictures of whatever mischief the Soviets were up to. Dwight Eisenhower denied such doings, a declaration that fell rather flat when the Russians produced the pilot, who had somehow survived. A big summit conference was axed, and Ike, somewhat red of countenance, finally canceled all U2 operations. (The Yanks eventually got Mr. Powers back by trading a captured Soviet spy for him.)

That U2 adventure was when we commoners realized the spy business had outgrown our comprehension.

Subsequently, the highdomes came up with these *unmanned* spy satellites that circled the earth 100 miles up, sending back detailed photos. Our guys predicted the Russian famine by zooming in on brown spots in Ukrainian wheat fields. They discovered poppy fields in Colombia and gold deposits in Brazil. It was like standing on the City Hall roof, looking south and getting the right time from a policeman's wristwatch in Waco. That's a little hard to grasp by those of us who can't find a sock in the dryer.

• • •

Therefore, it's difficult for us clods to understand this spy plane awkwardness. Supposedly, the U.S. "surveillance" plane was in "international airspace" when an "accident" occurred between a Chinese fighter plan and the Navy craft, resulting in the latter making an emergency landing on Chinese soil and creating a sticky situation indeed.

Now then, we thought the satellites were the spymasters, but here comes word that some spying is best done by common aircraft. And that our aviators have been eavesdropping on China, Russia and North Korea since the early days of the Cold War and that, in fact, several U.S. planes and lives have been silently lost, unbeknownst to CNN and headline writers.

This "international airspace," we are told, is sort of a Kings-X area where planes of all nationalities can fly at will, spying on each other to their little hearts' content, and nobody shoots.

Now, if Chinese fighter planes don't play by the rules, if they have a history of buzzing the big fat U.S. spycraft, we don't understand why something wasn't done about it before. And if the U.S. plane carried all this highly secret, valuable equipment, why would it be up there lumbering along by itself, subject to torment by Chinese hot pilots?

Surely, there is a logical, sophisticated answer to these technical conundrums, but it is far beyond our plebeian understanding. By the way, Mata Hari's real name was Margaretha Geertruida Zelle. Bet you didn't know that.

When We Got Dressed Up, We Needed a Place To Go

(Dallas Morning News, November 15, 2001)

Back in the dear dead days beyond recall, there was a back-woodsy description: "All dressed up and nowhere to go."

The phrase had obvious interpretation. Us hardy pioneers were a mite limited in such language flourishes as metaphor, oxymoron, and that ole debbil onomatopoeia. We needed—nay, demanded—simpler talk.

"All dressed up," etc., meant a fellow had gone to great pains to prepare for a party that didn't happen.

In those innocent times, when we got dressed up, there dang well better be some valid reason. We did not go gently back into overalls and brogans. If we were left waiting at the church—someone was dang sure gonna get his eye blacked.

And so it seemed for a while with this current world crisis. This country got itself attacked, thousands of innocents were killed, untold billions of tax dollars were spent, and The Great Unwashed was properly enraged. Patriotism swept the land, jaws became grimly set, and the exalted media genii deigned to join the commonfolk and lent their strong, clear tenors to "God Bless America" and such.

Our anger was fierce and unselfish, and we clutched fellow countrymen to our breasts and, united with brotherly outrage, charged the ramparts with bayonets fixed. And there was no one there. We were all dressed up, and there was no one to dance with.

As any old combat commander can tell you, fierce emotions are not applied or removed like makeup. You get your troops aroused, edgy, and angry on purpose, in anticipation of some unnatural motivation on the morrow.

Then, when tomorrow comes, and there's no apparent action, that antagonistic mood does not retreat quietly into its sheath, immediately ready to be summoned again. It turns within. The grunts find themselves barking at each other. They don't go to the mat, but their personalities remain on a combative edge.

Perhaps that's what happened for a while on these confused shores. Immediately after Terrible Tuesday, the populace worked up a fierce rage only to find the probable enemy disappearing in the mists. On the boob toob, we caught glimpses of bombers taking off from somewhere and troops boarding cargo planes somewhere. We saw constant reruns, from the files, of the presumed enemy in his beard and turban, squatting in the bush, testing an automatic rifle.

Until this week's wins at places like Mazar-e-Sharif and Kabul, little else seemed to happen in this weird war, except our leaders made the same pep rally speeches every time you turned around. And while they scrambled for encouraging words, we frequently turned on the nearest target, our own selves.

Who could imagine New York cops and firemen, those two heroic bands, in a physical scuffle at the disaster site? It happened. Arguments over overtime pay. How about the charities under fire, charges that donated dollars weren't reaching intended beneficiaries? Opportunistic con men scrounged around in search of financial gains from the emotional upheaval. Scam thy neighbor.

There has been the anthrax thing and billions involved in preventive measures. We had medics yelling that 20,000 Americans die from influenza each year, compared to four from anthrax, so how about some tax dollars for flu shots? Airlines got a $15 billion bailout from federal coffers, and other stricken businesses asked: Where's ours?

Then, of course, we had media wisemen reverting to their supervisory pedestals. A sailor fell off an aircraft carrier, and it led the newscast. "Thirteen civilians killed in bombing," a headline read. Some helicopter landing gear was found on a bleak plain, and it was a big story. This just in: Anthrax suspected on postcard in Bismarck, N.D.

Seemingly, the citizenship had all this steam worked up,

with no operative overflow valve. Now, with the positive news coming out of Afghanistan this week, perhaps we can revert to our original concept of who the real enemy is, and it's not supposed to be us.

Finest Hour? Is There Really Any Doubt?

(*Dallas Morning News,* May 31, 2001)

Far be it for a shade-tree historian to argue against the illustrious researchers of the boob tube, but there comes a time to square our tiny shoulders, stand up and be counted—as long as we don't have to stand up real straight, because that hurts back there somewhere.

Just the other day, some stentorian authority emerged from the set and offered hosannas to "America's finest hour." Nothing wrong with that; it has sort of a dramatic ring. The only objection is that it was applied to the 1991 Persian Gulf War. That raised the hackles of us old roosters who prefer that distinction for September 2, 1945, back before many of you were born.

The Gulf War (or Exxon Excursion, as some satirists call it) was respectable and all that and lasted a matter of days, even though our forces stopped a few miles short of total victory. Certainly, it set a record for patriotic parades back in the States, but America's finest hour? Come off it.

September 2, 1945, was the champion, no matter what the whippersnappers say. That was the day Japan gave up the towel, ending World War II after four years of shooting.

Of course, there were those soldiers and soldier families who thought of May 7, 1945, as America's finest hour, because it ended the long campaign in Europe. There was much celebrating around the land, as though the world had finally righted itself in favor of the good guys.

Some lads in the Pacific, however, noting the wild demonstrations in Times Square and other picnic grounds, thought the celebrations rather premature, since shells were still bursting in their immediate air.

• • •

At any rate, WWII, like that old suit in your closet, has

come back in style, thanks to commercial arts. The move was launched a couple of years back when Steven Spielberg filmed *Saving Private Ryan* amid a publicity campaign that had John Ringling North whirring in his crypt. TV newsman Tom Brokaw, while escorting veterans to a D-Day reunion in France, got the idea for a book, *The Greatest Generation,* which took up permanent residence on best-selling lists, prompting the author to compose another book on WWII participants and then another.

In the aftermath, some donors opened a WWII museum in New Orleans, which attracted passing fancy. Then, we had a lull until this *Pearl Harbor* extravaganza hit the movie scree, cunningly enough during Memorial Day weekend. Its promotion campaign was unrivaled. Two TV networks jumped on the bandwagon with special documentaries (one narrated by retired Gen. Norman Schwarzkopf) on that Japanese surprise attack.

• • •

Not only that, Congress has ordered a WWII memorial for the National Mall, apparently something on the style of the Vietnam Wall.

This has been in the hopper for eight years, but the location had been in dispute. Finally, President Bush reminded congressmen that they better get a move on: 1,100 WWII veterans were dying each day, and barely a third of the 16 million vets were still kicking. (One day last week, on *The Dallas Morning News'* obituary page, services were announced for eight WWII veterans, just in this immediate vicinity.)

You may expect the commercial parade to grow. In the copycat nature of the movie business, you can count on several other WWII films in the hopper. Some dress designers are trying to stimulate interest in fashions of the 1940s. New WWII photo albums and newspaper reproductions are on the market. Record albums of WWII songs are being offered. Who knows, maybe "The White Cliffs of Dover" will regain its rightful place, if Ding Dong Daddy or the Dixie Chicks record it.

However, there will remain some younger citizens who shrug at such history. The TV comedian Jay Leno recently took his microphone outside to interview passersby. In keeping with the current hullabaloo, Mr. Leno asked one young lady to identify Pearl Harbor. She said it was when the Spanish invaded America.

We Need to Keep This Rage

(September 27, 2001)

It is unhealthy, psychiatrists tell us, to keep anger bottled up. In Paul's Epistle to the Philippians, there is the counsel: "Let the sun not go down on your wrath."

Thomas De Quincey, a highdome of the early 1800s, agreed, "The grandest of all human sentiments? It is that man should forget his anger before he lies down to sleep."

It may seem impudent to question such authorities, but the suggestion here is that the September 11 anger not only be bottled but kept in a jug by the bed and a good swig taken every morning upon rising.

It may be most beneficial to the U.S. cause to sustain, in its original state, the wrath that swept the citizenry in the immediate aftermath of Terrible Tuesday. To diminish the national anger may be to diminish the nation's alertness or its eagerness to sacrifice.

The nature of a prosperous nation is to go about its business. The anger may be called up occasionally, even frequently, but each passing day—and there may be months and years of them—may subtract a wisp of the original rage.

To this shade-tree theorist, it is most important to keep the wrath alive and upfront. Uncle Sam needs to keep feeling violated and insulted. It is to this nation's benefit to retain a fierce and motivating anger, regardless how many pulpits that may offend.

• • •

In normal warfare, it is not so difficult to stay mad. In World War II, there were daily developments and dispatches from all over—a sea battle here, a beachhead there. Grandpa mounted a big map on the parlor wall and stayed by the radio, moving colored thumbtacks on the Philippines and North Africa, the better to monitor Allied progress or lack of same.

THE BIG, WIDE WORLD

Edward R. Murrow reported daily from London against a background of muddled explosions. In the newspapers, there were dispatches from Ernie Pyle and his typewriter tribe.

That particular war stayed very much alive, and even then, there were degrees of interest. The smart guys running the show were much aware of the importance of keeping the layman involved when he saw no smoke outside his window and heard no booms from the horizon. The Yanks at home needed heroes, and Colin Kelly and Butch O'Hare became matinee idols, and small boys, playing in the back yard, were Audie Murphy, Joe Foss and Pappy Boyington. There were bluebirds over the white cliffs of Dover, and the Andrew gals immortalized "The Boogie Woogie Bugle Boy of Company B."

There was an unspoken suspicion that Jimmy Doolittle's flamboyant 1942 strike on Tokyo actually was a propaganda blow for U.S. morale, moreso than sound military strategy. It was considered important to keep the at-home populace aroused and, excuse the expression, mad as hell.

• • •

In some ways, it shouldn't be difficult to maintain rage. This was a rape on our own front porch.

There first was terror, then horror, then sorrow, then patriotism and finally anger. But in the immediate aftermath, there was no further enemy action to feed the fire of rage. The populace was saturated with speeches, flag waving and politicians gathered on outside steps, giving interviews, singing songs and swearing allegiance to each other. But the homefolk need to sustain the anger; they need a focus for it, something real, not some vague terrorists whose names you can't pronounce.

There will be other mysterious outrages. Even the most optimistic did not think September 11 was the last of it. But when? And where and how? Waiting for the next shoe to fall breeds uneasiness, which may take precedence over wrath.

The country needs anger—not hatred, not a lynch-mob personality striking out at neighbors and storefronts, but a cool, contained lasting outrage. Mad is good. Long live mad.

We Pay a Price in War

(Dallas Morning News, January 10, 2002)

Chances are excellent that this premise will be taken the wrong way. For this, I apologize in advance, which ain't a bad idea for anyone trying to introduce a modest opinion.

But the fact that a soldier's death last week—one soldier—made such headlines in newspapers everywhere and was such a sensational news bulletin on TV newscasts is a commentary on this particular swamp we find ourselves mired in.

This is not to imply that any death is a minor occurrence. To the contrary. Death is intensely sad and personal. Sgt. Nathan Chapman was the Green Beret killed in an ambush in Afghanistan, and he suddenly became The Topic of the day. His family and background were immediately chronicled by dang near everyone with access to a keyboard or microphone. His photo, his family photo, and newsreel shots of his coffin were repeated incessantly.

The incident was treated, newswise, as though it were the tragedy of the century. In *The New York Times, The Chicago Tribune,* this newspaper, that newspaper, this cable news, that cable news, Sgt. Chapman became a familiar name, and his home, family and photo albums were researched as diligently as though he were a nominee for the Supreme Court. Cameras probed family and friends, perhaps to catch a chance tear or a choked voice. Media experts, expressions of deep concern on their wise countenances, gazed somberly into the cameras and seemed to be asking, "Why?" By gollies, somebody is guilty of something, and, by golly, somebody ought to pay.

● ● ●

As heartless as it may sound, perhaps it is time to remind the countryside that this business in the Middle East is war. W-a-r. And in any w-a-r, there are going to be casualties. It is the nature of the beast. There should be no shocked surprise. Read your history books.

The surprise, if any, is not that a Green Beret was killed but that he was the only fatality.

There was much ado about Sgt. Chapman being the "first U.S. soldier killed by enemy fire." Of course, a CIA interrogator named Mike Spann was killed in a Taliban prison riot on Nov. 25 and got his time in the media as the "first U.S. casualty" in that particular battlefield, but he wasn't a soldier per se.

Also, three Yank soldiers were killed by an errant U.S. bomb, and seven others died in accidents, but they didn't receive nearly as much attention, despite being just as much a war casualty as any. Can you name one? Apparently, it isn't that newsworthy to be killed by a falling crane.

"There are others who have died over there," said Sgt. Chapman's mom, "and they're just as much heroes as him." There's a grieving lady but one with an honest perspective.

• • •

From *The Washington Post:* "The attack, which some officials characterized as an ambush, underscored the continued danger and challenges facing U.S. forces in Afghanistan as they attempt to track down remnants of the al-Qaeda terror network and its Taliban allies."

Well, fellows, there will be continued danger and challenges. That's hardly a headline. There were dangers and challenges at Iwo Jima, Omaha Beach, and Bunker Hill. There were dangers and challenges at Guam, the Argonne Forest, and the Anzio beachhead. There were victims in the wake of the USS *Indianapolis,* Maggot Beach at Guadalcanal, and the Hindenburg Line.

In war, there are casualties. They are not welcome, but they are expected. It is the price we have chosen to pay, regardless of the second-guessers in their nice, clean, safe, offices expressing shock and, yes, national resentment that an Army sergeant should die in an enemy ambush. It seems to stun some news folk that they ain't playing with popguns over there.

Always Time for Another Shoe to Drop

(*Dallas Morning News,* February 28, 2002)

Let's look at the scoreboard. Two down and a half-dozen to go. Or is it three down and a dozen to go? It is all according to who is classifying likely terrorist targets in this land.

Remember, it was the Super Bowl that supposedly led the hit list. Seventy-three thousand giddy Yanks all in one place for an event televised in 200 countries. For that one day, Feb. 3, the stage seemed ideal for the next terrorist attack on these shores.

All the smarts, from President Bush on down, are convinced that Mideast terrorists are not finished with their dirty work. But where and when? Since September, we have waited nervously for the next shoe to fall.

What if the Washington guardians had ignored the Super Bowl and another September 11 had indeed occurred? Our security forces took a public threshing for their failure to foresee the World Trade Center and Pentagon acts. They could ill afford another tragic embarrassment of being caught with their pants at half-mast.

So the fed watchdogs narrowed their eyes, loosened their holsters and brought an army of grim security experts to New Orleans at a cost that would feed Somalia for a year. And this isn't to poke ridicule at the alarm. There was no other choice.

• • •

Back in November, of course, we had the World Series and all its attention and its crowds in New York and Phoenix. But that was too soon after the Trade Center attack, and our leaders had yet to project the future. But now our snoops supposedly have established contacts in dim, sinister corners of the world and are convinced we ain't seen nothing yet.

A study by the Heritage Homeland Security Task Force, which Ed Meese co-chairs, saw September 11 as a signal from the terrorists:

"Their war against America would no longer be confined to such overseas targets as embassies or to U.S. servicemen on ships like the USS *Cole*. Instead, they would take their war to America's heartland, killing as many innocent civilians as they could with any means at their disposal—first to change U.S.A. policy and ultimately to destroy American and Western civilization."

CIA Director George Tenet warned that "high-profile events, such as the Olympics or Super Bowl, fit the terrorists' interest in striking another blow within the United States that would command worldwide media attention."

· · ·

With the Super Bowl passing peacefully, attention centered on the Salt Lake Games, which had even more of an international audience. However, come to think of it, any attack on the Olympics might include foreign visitors and participants among its victims, some from countries with a moderate attitude on terrorism. This might cause more nations to take more active roles against the al-Qaeda cause.

Anyways, we couldn't afford the chance. Again, we saddled our posses and sent them to Utah at a possible cost of $400 million. Again, it was a wild goose chase but a necessary one. We are going to be chasing a lot of wild geese for goodness knows how long.

Remember, there was an official warning from Washington that something bad was going to happen on February 12. Supposedly, this came from an inside tip or from documents left behind by departing forces in Afghanistan.

This may bring a suspicion from us shade-tree experts: How do we know these tips, or documents left behind by fleeing al-Qaeda, weren't planted just to cause the United States more tension—and expense?

After all, isn't that one of Osama bin Laden's main objectives—to diminish America's wealth? And what if false seeds were planted that the next target would be a big sports event with international TV exposure? What if the next attack instead is a bomb quietly aimed at a hinterland dam that furnishes power for millions?

The only conclusion we may draw is that there is no conclusion, not right now. We may as well learn to sleep with one eye open. To do otherwise is to have a blind and foolish trust that the last shoe has fallen. It is enough to keep a nation both nervous and angry, and that may not be all bad.